Hike Maryland

Other Guides by Bryan MacKay

Cycle Maryland

Paddle Maryland

Hike
MARYLAND

A GUIDE to the Scenic Trails
of the Free State

Bryan MacKay

Photographs by Debi and Bryan MacKay
Maps by Bill Nelson

JOHNS HOPKINS UNIVERSITY PRESS · BALTIMORE

© 2018 Johns Hopkins University Press
All rights reserved. Published 2018
Printed in the United States of America on acid-free paper
9 8 7 6 5 4 3 2 1

Johns Hopkins University Press
2715 North Charles Street
Baltimore, Maryland 21218-4363
www.press.jhu.edu

Library of Congress Cataloging-in-Publication Data

Names: MacKay, Bryan, author.
Title: Hike Maryland : A Guide to the Scenic Trails of the Free State /
    Bryan MacKay ; Photographs by Debi and Bryan MacKay ; Maps by Bill Nelson.
Description: Baltimore, Maryland : Johns Hopkins University Press, 2018. |
    Includes index.
Identifiers: LCCN 2017030360| ISBN 9781421424989 (pbk. : alk. paper) |
    ISBN 1421424983 (pbk. : alk. paper) | ISBN 9781421424996 (electronic) |
    ISBN 1421424991 (electronic)
Subjects: LCSH: Hiking—Maryland—Guidebooks. | Maryland—Guidebooks.
Classification: LCC GV199.42.M3 M34 2018 | DDC 796.5109752—dc23
    LC record available at https://lccn.loc.gov/2017030360

A catalog record for this book is available from the British Library.

Special discounts are available for bulk purchases of this book. For more information,
please contact Special Sales at 410-516-6936 or specialsales@press.jhu.edu.

Johns Hopkins University Press uses environmentally friendly book materials,
including recycled text paper that is composed of at least 30 percent post-consumer
waste, whenever possible.

Contents

🐾 = Dogs allowed. Check park rules for leash requirements.

Preface

Welcome to *Hike Maryland*. This book is the culmination of my fifty years of experience exploring the unique and wonderful natural areas of our state. During that time, I've done quite a bit of hiking in these and other places. I can't think of one hike that I did not enjoy, but some venues stand out for their scenic beauty, abundant or unique plant and animal life, or their contribution to the natural and historic heritage of Maryland. Such places merit greater recognition and deserve a wider appreciation by the public for their value for conservation, education, and the quality of our shared life as Maryland citizens. I wrote this book for these reasons. I hope you will enjoy reading it, use it often to hike the trails described, and maybe even learn something from it regarding our natural heritage.

Maryland has many advantages for the hiker. Geographically, it extends from the ocean to the mountains, and both are within a three-hour drive for the majority of the state's residents. Maryland has a great diversity of natural habitats and is home to a large number of plants and animals. The variety of outdoor experiences available to citizens is nothing short of amazing. Finally, Maryland has an excellent system of public lands available for hiking, including national parks, state parks and forests, and even privately owned tracts open to the public.

For this book, I have selected the *best* natural areas Maryland has to offer, truly special places that represent the scenic beauty of the Free State. Each has some outstanding characteristic that calls me to return again and again. Whether it's a path leading to a scenic vista, a trail through a state-designated wildland where a hiker can experience a sense of solitude, a place with exceptional displays of wildflowers, birds, or other seasonal biological phenomena, or a walk through habitats that are rare or even unique, every hike is certain to delight you in some way. The text is designed to illuminate what makes these places so interesting and valuable. In an era where much basic information is available online and social media promotes opinion unencumbered by expertise and experience, *Hike Maryland* is a book whose added value lies in enlightening text based on my years of experience in the field.

Hike Maryland deals only with natural areas. There are no amusement parks, festival sites, museums, quaint villages, historic inns, or superb restaurants described and listed. Such day-trip destinations have already been well covered by other authors.

Accompanying each trip description is an essay that considers a relevant organism or related concept in greater detail. I have tried to enhance descriptions of life histories with interesting new findings gleaned from the recent scientific literature. Some of these essays provide a closer look at a particular aspect of conservation in Maryland and offer a perspective on controversial issues with suggestions for future action on the part of society.

Each chapter includes a trail map that shows significant roads and parking areas, in addition to the trail itself. Written directions at the end of each trip description will get you to the trailhead from the Baltimore-Washington metropolitan area. A street address is included (where a usable one exists) as are GPS coordinates for the trailhead. Note that handheld GPS units are not always reliable on trails sited in valleys with steep-sided mountains. Similarly, cell phone coverage is intermittent or nonexistent on some of these trails, especially those in the western counties of Maryland (but it's a good idea to carry a fully charged cell phone nonetheless).

Hikers often enjoy bringing their favorite canine companion on nature walks. I've noted at the beginning of each hike whether dogs are allowed, and if they must be kept on leash. (This is also indicated by an icon 🐾 in the table of contents.) In the few areas where leashes are not required, I still recommend you leash your dogs. You don't want them to chase wildlife and possibly end up injured, nor would you want them to run through poison ivy and later transfer it to you. By keeping dogs leashed and on the trails you can avoid their trampling on fragile wildflowers. Perhaps most importantly, it is a courtesy to other hikers to restrain your pets. Even if dogs are allowed on a particular trail, it doesn't always mean they will have a good experience. I urge you to read the hike description (terrain and length) before making your decision to bring Fido along.

Individuals in wheelchairs or with other physical challenges and parents with children in strollers will find only a few of these hikes suitable. One short but quite accessible trail is the Great Falls Tavern walk. Other trails that might be suitable but have a sandy or gravelly trail surface and some degree of slope include the C&O Canal towpath, the Red Trail at Calvert Cliffs State Park, portions of the Susquehanna River Trail, the Muddy Creek Falls Trail at Swallow Falls State Park, and the initial mile of the Kendall Trail. Even on these trails, pushing a wheeled conveyance like a stroller or wheelchair will require considerable effort. Note, however, that almost every paved multi-use recreational trail described in the companion book to this volume, *Cycle Maryland*, is eminently suitable for persons using wheelchairs or pushing strollers or for individuals on crutches.

I hope you enjoy using this book as you explore Maryland. May you have many safe and memorable experiences in your journeys.

Acknowledgments

Having spent more than fifty years hiking in many of Maryland's most interesting and unusual natural areas, I am indebted to the many friends, acquaintances, and students who have accompanied me on these journeys of discovery. Early on, Charley Stine showed me several of the best places, in terms of ecological value, and enlightened me about the unusual plants and animals living there. Along with members of the Chesapeake Audubon Society, we had a great time on these weekend field trips. In the 1980s, I taught "Field Biology of Maryland," hiking several of the trails included in this book, teaching and learning about their ecology; I appreciate my employer of thirty-four years, the University of Maryland Baltimore County (UMBC), for giving me the opportunity to offer this course in the summer sessions. Similarly, I have taken well over one hundred of my plant biology classes to Soldiers Delight Natural Environment Area for walking "ecotours" of this unique landscape. Often, a teacher will learn as much as his students on such excursions, and for this I am grateful.

In 1992, a (fairly) young and definitely naïve version of me first approached Johns Hopkins University Press regarding possible publication of a guidebook to venues for hiking, cycling, and canoeing in Maryland. I am indebted to the Press, and my long-time editor, Bob Brugger, for immediately accepting the manuscript and shepherding it through publication and sales. To date, that book has sold more than 21,000 copies, and it has been gratifying to receive so many compliments on it from people who love the outdoors. Now that book about the best places to go in Maryland for hiking, cycling, and paddling has received a fresh interpretation with the publication of three separate guidebooks, each devoted exclusively to a single sport. Each venue has been revisited and viewed with a fresh eye and the text revised. New venues have been added. Information about nature has been updated. I believe these new books improve significantly on the older one; I have written the book I want to grab when I leave the house for a day of hiking on one of Maryland's most scenic trails. I appreciate my present editor at the Press, Catherine Goldstead, for her vision about this project and her steady hand at guiding it to fruition. I am also indebted to Mary Lou Kenney for her copyediting expertise.

I am especially grateful that my wife, Debi MacKay, loves to hike with me as much as I enjoy her company, especially for those trails visited in 2016 when I wrote the bulk of the text. Debi is undaunted by long days afield, difficult trails, rain, sleet, cold, heat, humidity, and my frequent stops to examine some interesting plant or creature. Debi always carries her camera, and several of the photographs that enhance the text are hers.

Others who have recently accompanied me on hikes undertaken specifically for this book, or who have provided information, include Ruth Bergstrom, Scott Campbell (Savage River State Forest), Steve Carr (Maryland Department of Natural Resources), Dave Curson, April Foiles, Tom Giannaccini, Tim Houghton, Bill Hulslander (Assateague Island National Seashore), Frode Jacobsen, Mark Scallion, and Rodger Waldmann. I have often used the website of the Maryland Biodiversity project (www.marylandbiodiversity.com) for information on the distributions of plants and animals in our state; thanks to founders Bill Hubick and Jim Brighton.

Maps for this book have been prepared by Bill Nelson of Bill Nelson Maps: I thank him for his expertise.

While any author receives and appreciates help with a writing project, he is ultimately responsible for any errors and omissions. Should you find any you wish to tell me about, I can be contacted through Johns Hopkins University Press.

Fifty Years of Hiking in Maryland

I've been hiking the trails of Patapsco Valley State Park, near my lifelong home, for more than fifty years. That's a half century, a not inconsiderable stretch of time that allows some reflection and perspective regarding how trails, the hiking experience, and the surrounding forest have changed. And while so many of my hikes have been in Patapsco, it's really not so parochial. Patapsco mirrors the delights and problems of many of the trails in central Maryland, close to the population centers of the Old Line State.

Hiking was a popular activity in Patapsco right from the start. When the Patapsco Forest Reserve was designated in 1907 it was Maryland's first tract in what later became the Maryland State Park system. In those early years, families camped for most of the summer at the Orange Grove area, swimming, hiking, and rusticating in an effort to ameliorate the heat and humidity of Baltimore City summers.

Arguably the most significant change to Maryland parks in general and Patapsco in particular occurred during the Great Depression of the 1930s. The Civilian Conservation Corps (CCC) built an astonishing amount of infrastructure in Maryland state parks, as well as federally owned parks, including picnic shelters, roads, cabins, and so on. The CCC boys also built trails, many of which are still in use. The alert hiker can often detect stone reinforcing walls, culverts, bridges, springhead boxes, and other such improvements, invariably built out of the local stone. Almost a century on, the positive improvements for Maryland hikers made by the CCC cannot be overstated.

The 1980s was a decade of change for Maryland hikers, trails, and the surrounding forest. In particular, one technological advance changed the trail experience forever: the mountain bike. Within a decade, trail use by cyclists went from zero to the point where on some backcountry trails in Patapsco I sometimes saw more mountain bikers than hikers. Trails changed from narrow footpaths to wider trails packed smooth and hard. Some trails that had been fine for the occasional hiker proved to be erosion-prone with heavy use. A few mountain bikers took it upon themselves to carve out new "renegade" trails through previously untrammeled forest. And hikers out to experience the peace of nature found their reveries interrupted by hard-charging mountain bikers focused on their adrenaline-fed sport. Thankfully, this period did not last long, as mountain bikers soon realized they needed to improve their public image and also give back to the parks that hosted their activities. Today, in my experience, most riders are friendly and courteous to hikers, many poorly sited and erodible trails have been relocated, and much, perhaps a majority, of volunteer trail maintenance in state parks is done by the mountain bike community. Relations between hikers and cyclists are now largely positive, through the good offices of both parties. The mountain bike brought change to Maryland trails, but it was not a particularly negative change.

That same decade of the 1980s brought another major change to many Maryland trails, although it is perhaps not especially well recognized even today. Most hiking trails pass through forest, and the character of that forest has been altered visibly in the last thirty years. Over most of Maryland, the number of white-tailed deer increased exponentially between 1985 and 2000. Seventy years ago, a successful deer hunter was so uncommon that he might find his picture in the local paper. In 1976, the deer harvest (which is correlated with the population size) was less than 10,000 animals; in the decade starting in 2010, almost ten times as many deer were taken by sport hunters. Today, it is difficult to hike in central Maryland without seeing one or more white-tails. Why is this huge increase in white-tailed deer numbers of importance to hikers? Two reasons: effects on vegetation and an increase in the tick population.

First, deer eat incredible quantities of vegetation. Most forests in central Maryland exhibit a "browse line," a point about five feet off the ground, below which little or nothing green remains. Squat and you can often see for a hundred yards through the forest. But visit a forest where deer numbers are in balance with their environment and low vegetation will block your view within a few yards. This change has been so gradual that many hikers have been unaware of it. In many Maryland forests, there are few if any seedling trees; for example, in the Prettyboy Reservoir watershed in Baltimore County, more than 80 percent of study plots had no tree regeneration. Without replacement trees in the understory, mature trees lost to storms or insects will create light gaps in the forest that will dry soils, allow invasion by non-natives, and disturb nutrient cycling.

Also impacted are forest wildflowers. Many herbaceous plants are becoming more and more rare. For the hiker, locations where a particular species of wildflower is fondly recalled are now barren. For example, one study found that 26 percent of white trillium plants in the study area had been eaten by white-tailed deer. I have personally seen summer forest wildflowers like Culver's root and white baneberry become less common and spring ephemerals like mayapple with no leaves and a browsed stem.

The second way in which the population explosion of white-tailed deer affects hikers is that they host black-legged ticks, commonly known as deer ticks. These ticks, in turn, can transmit Lyme disease to humans. Lyme disease was first noted in the mid-1970s and formally described by science in 1981. The number of Lyme disease cases in Maryland increased rapidly during the same years the deer population was increasing exponentially. Since 2000, when statewide deer populations began to increase at a much slower rate, Lyme cases have held relatively constant. (Actual numbers of Lyme disease cases reported by the Centers for Disease Control and Prevention is inaccurate; in 2015, the CDC admitted that the real number of cases may be as much as ten times what they report. They now believe that there are almost 300,000 case of Lyme disease nationwide each year, making it the most significant vector-borne disease in the northern hemisphere.)

What this means for hikers is that it is unwise to walk through heavy brush or anywhere that low vegetation touches your body. A tick check is mandatory after any hike. It is now considered sensible to wear a long-sleeved shirt and long pants tucked into socks, even in hot weather. Use of an insect repellent on pants and socks is also recommended. Not every tick is a deer tick (dog ticks are also quite common in Maryland), and not every deer tick carries the Lyme bacteria (and it takes at least twenty-four hours of attachment to your body for an infected tick to transmit the bacteria), but avoiding ticks is a far better strategy than dealing with their bites. Lest this information make you want to confine your hiking to the local shopping mall, realize that reasonable precautions should keep you tick- and Lyme-free.

In the past decade, technology has changed the hiking experience. Handheld GPS devices are excellent (although sometimes unreliable in steep mountainous terrain). Online trail maps are readily available and may be accessed by cell phone, at least where coverage is available. All of which raises the question: why are printed guidebooks like this one even necessary? My goal in writing this book is to advise the reader about the *best* places to hike in Maryland from among a large number of possible venues. The text explains *why* these places are special. Everyone loves beautiful or dramatic scenery, but not everyone is aware of the exceptional value of certain places for conservation, biological diversity, and ecological services.

Social media has in some ways changed the hiking experience of late. It provides an opportunity to meet and hike with like-minded people, can provide up-to-date information on trail conditions, and may even provide opinions regarding trails that might fit your hiking style along with distance and difficulty estimations. I've met any number of groups while hiking; invariably, when everyone is under the age of forty, the group has assembled via an online social media platform. In contrast, traditional hiking clubs like the Mountain Club of Maryland and the Sierra Club tend to be populated with older individuals, or at least a mix of ages.

But at its heart, hiking is about as simple an athletic endeavor as there is, requiring no special equipment except a comfortable pair of shoes. No amount of technology can enhance the feeling of freedom and peace that comes from spending time in nature. The flute song of a wood thrush at dusk, the delicate fragrance of a summer wildflower, the sweet feel of a spring breeze on your skin—these are all gifts to us hikers from the natural world we live in. And that, my friends, is why we hike, why I wrote this guidebook, and why I hope you enjoy reading and using it. Happy Trails!

Hike Maryland

Assateague Island National Seashore: North Beach

County: Worcester

Distance: Up to 5 miles one way; out-and-back hike

Difficulty: Moderate to strenuous. Flat; sandy terrain

Dogs: Prohibited

Why It's Special: A natural and wild ocean beach with excellent wildlife watching opportunities (especially birdwatching)

More Information: Assateague Island State Park, http://dnr.maryland.gov /publiclands/Pages/eastern/assateague.aspx, (410) 641-2120. Assateague Island National Seashore, www.nps.gov/asis, (410) 641-1441

Street Address: Assateague Island National Seashore, 7206 National Seashore Lane, Berlin, MD 21811

GPS Coordinates: 38.247595, 75.154568 (National Seashore Visitor Center)

Assateague Island forms the easternmost boundary of Maryland. A barrier island separated from the mainland by a shallow coastal bay, Assateague is a study in contrasts. To the north is Ocean City, an intensively developed vacation destination with the highest population density in the state on holiday summer weekends. Just across the inlet, much of the upper five miles of Assateague exists as de facto wilderness, where visitors are few in number and minimal in their impact. Protected by Assateague Island National Seashore and Assateague Island State Park, this land of sand and sea is a special and enticing place.

Beachwalking is a familiar seashore activity, but few places on the East Coast have as long a stretch of truly deserted beach as

Assateague. For this reason, a natural community of plants and animals dominates the life of Assateague, and we humans are only temporary visitors and observers. For anyone interested in the natural world, especially in birds, there are few better places in Maryland. Even if you just want to get away from it all, Assateague is a great place to hike.

A note of caution: this ten-mile out-and-back walk is a long and difficult hike if completed in its entirety. Walking over sand is more tiring than walking over almost any other type of surface. In summer the beach can be very hot, although heatstroke can be easily avoided by taking occasional swims in the ocean. Bring lots of sunblock to avoid burning. Be sure to carry at least two quarts of drinking water per person; in addition to the heat and lack of shade, salt spray and a constant breeze can be desiccating. Insect repellent is a must if you plan to explore the area behind the dunes; the regular southerly breeze usually keeps the winged hordes at bay on the forebeach. So come prepared, especially if you bring children.

Trip Description

Begin your hike from the day-use parking lot of Assateague Island State Park, operated by Maryland's Department of Natural Resources. There is parking here for hundreds of cars, usually sufficient if you arrive before 11 a.m. or after 4 p.m. in beach season and always ample at other times of the year. An entrance fee is charged. Changing houses with warm-water showers, flush toilets, drinking water, and a seasonal snack bar are available.

Unlike most of the other hikes in this book, this one offers you the chance to see lots of wildlife even before you leave the parking lot. A small contingent of the Assateague pony herd often patrols the parking lot for handouts, soliciting donations of food as their own special token of admission and leaving the unwary with a fragrant reminder of their visit wedged in shoe soles, on sandal bottoms, or between the toes. Most visitors are enchanted by the famous ponies, and a few minutes of observation will reveal the degree of poor judgment of which humans are capable in their effort to experience wildlife up close and personal. Although the ponies are generally docile, they can become quite persistent in their pursuit of food and may be short-tempered and even aggressive on occasion. Ponies kick and

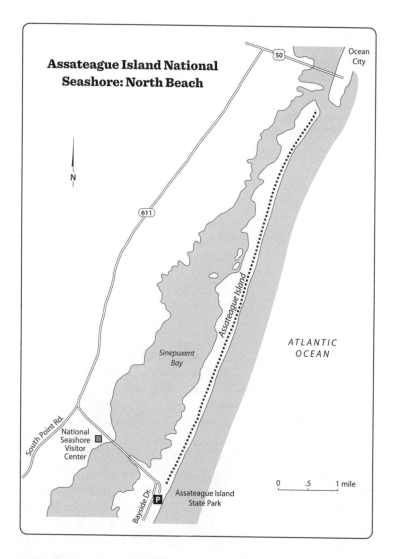

bite, so avoid feeding them (it's against park regulations) and keep your distance. The parking lot is also frequented by gulls (mostly laughing gulls in the summer and ring-billed gulls in the winter), crows, and grackles, all of whom will scavenge shamelessly through the accumulated trash discarded by your fellow visitors. Although all of this animal activity is artificially induced by us humans, the parking lot is nevertheless a great place to observe behavior. Students of ethology will have few other opportunities to ply their trade from the comfort of an air-conditioned automobile.

Walk toward the beach, crossing the dunes on the boardwalk provided. Despite the presence of this boardwalk, a few thoughtless people have created their own footpaths over the dunes. Such actions compact the shallow soil, kill the fragile vegetation, and make the dune more susceptible to erosion by wind and water.

At the ocean's edge, turn left (north). Five miles of ocean beach stretch in front of you, becoming increasingly less populated the farther you walk. Indeed, in colder weather you may be the only person in sight. As you walk north, notice the substantial dunes that have been built up near the bathing beach. This continuous battlement, known as the primary dune, protects the inner stretches of the island from the pounding surf during storm events. These dunes are not natural. Bulldozers built them up years ago, and the dunes are repaired whenever a breakthrough occurs. In the winter, when strong winds may erode the dunes, snow fences are erected to catch the airborne sand.

The tops of well-established dunes have been colonized by vegetation, dominated by dunegrass, *Ammophila breviligulata*. The most important plant on Assateague Island, this insignificant-looking grass acts as a living snow fence, combing sand out of the air. Grains that hit the blade are funneled downward by the shallow V shape and accumulate around the base. In most plants, this act of self-burial would be suicidal, but dunegrass thrives in this situation. In fact, it grows vigorously only when continually buried, spreading via underground rhizomes. Roots reach downward to the water table far below, further stabilizing the plant. If you look closely at the stem, you'll see that crystals of salt accumulate here. In many less hardy plants, this would be the literal kiss of death, as the salt would draw water out of the plant's tissues. In *Ammophila*, however, the blade is composed of parallel ridges of impervious tissue where the salt crystals accumulate, while the more sensitive soft tissues occupy the hollows. Dunegrass is a common food plant for the Assateague ponies.

The dunes are actively maintained only where they protect man-made structures in the state park and national seashore. Elsewhere, the dunes are allowed to erode, build up, or migrate, as the vagaries of nature dictate. For this reason, the solid wall of dunes soon gives way to occasional breakouts and then single isolated dunes as you hike northward.

Dune erosion occurs naturally on a frequent, if irregular, basis. Winter storms, with strong winds and large storm surges, can flatten dunes and even wash over the entire width of the island. Although not as violent as hurricanes, winter storms, popularly known as nor'easters, may last for several days and can be almost equally destructive.

As you walk along the beach, you will no doubt see an assortment of small shorebirds foraging at the water's edge. These amusing little animals scurry along just out of reach of advancing waves and follow retreating water seaward for a few moments until the next wave arrives. Identification of the shorebirds is rarely easy, even for experienced birders, and mixed flocks of sandpiper-like birds are often just called "peeps," for their distinctive calls. The two largest shorebirds you are likely to see in summer, however, are easy to recognize. Both are about the size of crows. The willet is rather nondescript until it flies, then revealing a distinctive black and white banding pattern on the underside of the wing and almost invariably uttering its "pill-will-willet" call. Willets nest in the salt marshes behind Assateague. The other distinctive large shorebird, the oystercatcher, is far less common, so count it as a real find when you see one. Oystercatchers are mostly black but have bright orange bills and a yellow eye ring. As their name suggests, they are most often found feeding in shallow oyster beds like those off Chincoteague, but on occasion they will stray out onto the beach. Although shorebirds are present at Assateague year-round, diversity and numbers are greatest during the spring and fall migrations. May is the peak month for spring migrations, whereas fall migrants arrive as early as mid-July and continue passing through for the next two months.

Shorebirds are the most distinctive animals you're likely to see on this walk, but other, smaller life forms are found in the zone between the ocean and the dunes. The intertidal zone, where the shorebirds feed, has some interesting residents. The mole crab is a common one. This small crustacean swims in on the leading edge of a wave; as the wave recedes, it rapidly buries itself in the wet sand, facing the beach. The mole crab then raises its periscopes: a pair of eyes on the ends of long stalks, a set of antennae that forms a snorkel for breathing, and a feathery set of appendages that seine the next incoming wave for animal and vegetable matter. On occasion, you may see another resident of the intertidal zone: *Donax*, the coquina clam. These tiny, brightly colored clams glisten in the sun momentarily before they, too, burrow in the sand. They siphon the incoming waves for food. Coquina clams may be rare or incredibly plentiful, depending on the abundance of their parasites and predators at any given time.

The sun-blasted beach above the high-tide mark is an even harsher environment for plants and animals than the intertidal zone. Fresh water is all but nonexistent, and the food supply can be highly variable. You're likely to run across only two kinds of animals here, both of whom feed on detritus—dead plant and animal matter. If you lie down on the beach, especially in late afternoon and while you're wet, you may notice tiny animals that hop about on your skin like jumping beans. These are beach hoppers (also known as beach fleas). They are amphipod crustaceans, with blue eyes and well-developed forelegs for jumping.

By far the most interesting resident of the forebeach, however, is the ghost crab. This drab, sand-colored crab ranges in size from immature, thumbnail-size specimens to husky individuals three inches across the shell. Ghost crabs live in burrows on the forebeach, notable for the scrabbling tracks in the vicinity laid down by the occupant. These burrows may be several feet deep, providing the crab with the cool, moist environment needed for survival. Although you may see ghost crabs during the day, scurrying sideways over the sand, night is when they are most active and most easily observed. By late summer, when the year's crop of juveniles swell the population, an evening stroll along the beach will reveal a density of several crabs per square foot, as far as the eye can see. They will (almost) always avoid your footfall but will crawl across your foot if you stand in place. Ghost crabs feed on almost anything they can find, alive or dead; they are true omnivores.

Ghost crabs are among the most terrestrial of the world's many crab species, but they are still water dependant. They have large gills that must be kept wet to pass oxygen to the bloodstream, and their deep burrows are very humid, preserving moisture. Ghost crabs lay eggs in the surf, and the larvae develop at sea.

The northern portion of Assateague Island is almost devoid of dunes. Large areas of hard-packed sand, studded with cobbles and flotsam, stretch from ocean to bayside. These are known as wash-over flats and, as their name implies, result from salt water incursions during major storms. The salt water kills the sparse vegetation, making the sand more susceptible to wind and water erosion. Once a washover flat is established, it is very difficult to convert it into a dune-protected beach.

Washover flats are, however, important habitats for some species of nesting shorebirds. Mixed colonies of terns, gulls, plovers, and skimmers nest communally here, taking advantage of the lack of human traffic and the long sight lines along which predators can be spotted and driven off. These species are extraordinarily sensitive to disturbance, and a casual stroll through one of these colonies may be enough to kill many nestlings by trampling or cause abandonment. Predatory gulls often hover nearby, waiting for the opportunity to swoop down on unprotected eggs and nestlings. Therefore, confine your walking to the intertidal zone when hiking here in the nesting season, late April through early August.

At last, after five miles of walking, you will run out of beach almost in the shadow of Ocean City. The contrast is remarkable. You are separated from Ocean City by a channelized inlet only a few hundred yards across. Created by the great storm of 1933, it must be regularly dredged to keep it open for the fishing and recreational fleet of West Ocean City. Currents here are swift and irregular, so avoid swimming anywhere near this end of the island.

The northern end of Assateague Island is several hundred feet west of the southern tip of Ocean City and is considerably narrower in width. The huge jetty at Ocean City interrupts the southerly flow of sand in the Atlantic, depositing it on the bathing beaches but robbing Assateague of its sandy lifeblood. Barrier islands like Assateague are dynamic, shifting landward or seaward depending on whether the forces of erosion or sand accumulation dominate. But the northern tip of Assateague has moved only westward toward the mainland in the last sixty years, and scientists expect that the island may fuse with the mainland sometime in the next century.

As with all out-and-back hikes, you have now reached only the halfway point, so retrace your steps back to the state park. Fortunately, there are always new sights to see and novel discoveries to make on the return trip.

Directions

From Baltimore or Washington, cross the Bay Bridge and continue south on Route 50 through Easton, Cambridge, and Salisbury. Just before the bridge to Ocean City, turn right on Route 611 at the prominent sign marking the Assateague Island National Seashore. Follow Route 611 for 5.8 miles. Just before crossing the bridge onto Assateague Island, be sure to stop at the Visitor Center, where there are interesting displays, information, ranger-led talks, drinking water, and flush toilets. To reach the trailhead parking lot, continue straight ahead over the Verrazano Bridge to the entrance kiosk for Assateague Island State Park. A fee is charged. Park in the bathing beach parking lot straight ahead.

Other Outdoor Recreational Opportunities Nearby

Camping facilities are available at both the state park and the national seashore. The state park has hot-water showers and flush toilets; it is so popular that reservations are a must. The national seashore sites have only portable toilets and cold-water showers. In hot weather, a screen house is a virtual necessity, providing refuge from the sun and bugs. Because of the physical discomfort of camping on the beach, consider camping at the Shad Landing area of Pocomoke River State Park, about a forty-five-minute commute away.

It is possible to walk the many miles of beach south of the state park. If you're interested in solitude or nature, however, forget it. Bathers dominate the beach near campgrounds, while surf fishermen in oversand vehicles occupy the beach at regular intervals south to the Virginia line.

For bicyclists, a ten-mile paved bike path traverses the length of the developed part of Assateague Island.

Paddling a canoe or kayak in the back bay (Assawoman Bay) of Assateague Island can be pleasant if it's not too windy and you stay close to the shore. Seasonal rentals are available at the Old Ferry Landing in the National Seashore.

PIPING PLOVERS

The month of May on Assateague Island is a busy time, with life returning to the wide sand beaches and washover flats. Birds swirl overhead: gulls, terns, plovers, willets, and sandpipers, many of them nesting alone or in colonies on the deserted sand, far from human disturbance. One species, the uncommon and diminutive piping plover, has an influence on beach regulations and the hiker experience far beyond what one would expect based on its tiny size and rarity. Between mid-April and about mid-July, foot travel on Assateague's North Beach is limited to the intertidal zone in order to permit piping plovers to nest, incubate eggs, and raise chicks to fledging. The United States Fish and Wildlife Service lists piping plovers as "threatened," a designation that requires management of the birds' habitat so as to maximize their chances of reproductive success.

Piping plovers are small, rather nondescript shorebirds that resemble a number of sandpiper species referred to by frustrated beginning birders as "peeps." Piping plovers are pale, with feathers similar in color to dry beach sand. They have yellow-orange legs, a yellow bill with a black tip, a white rump, and a black partial collar. Piping plovers migrate, overwintering in the southern United States and the Bahamas.

In 1986, when piping plovers were added to the federal Endangered Species list, there were just 790 breeding pairs on the Atlantic coast. (There is a smaller, disjunct population found near the Great Lakes.) After three decades of intensive regulatory protection of their nesting beaches, that number of breeding pairs has more than doubled to just under 2,000, and the total population is estimated at about 8,000 birds. At Assateague, there has been on average about 42 pairs, each of whom usually produce just one fledged offspring each year. But piping plovers typically lay four eggs to a clutch. Why the low birth rate? The high mortality is blamed on natural causes like predation and weather. While most piping plovers nest on North Beach, a few colonize the dozen miles of coast to the south, between the campgrounds and the Virginia border. Despite the fact that oversand vehicles

(continued)

are permitted on this stretch of beach, piping plover reproductive success has been surprisingly good, with a high of almost three young fledged per breeding pair in 2014. Closure of some beaches to oversand vehicles for the protection of piping plovers and other nesting shorebirds has been controversial, especially in North Carolina, but Marylanders seem to accept North Beach closures without much fuss.

Piping plovers nest singly on the open beach, typically on sand or washover gravel with shells, pebbles, wrack, or beachgrass nearby. Three to five eggs are laid in late April and May and are incubated for twenty-seven days. During this time, adult piping plovers will actively defend their nest, attacking predators and using a broken-wing display to lead human intruders away from the eggs. The young are precocial, running about actively soon after hatching. Fledging takes another month, a time when predation is common. Foxes, raccoons, crows, and even ghost crabs are the major causes of egg and nestling loss at Assateague. In an effort to reduce predation, scientists have on occasion placed exclosures (fences of mesh wire with a ceiling of monofilament fishing line) over some of the nests on the island. Although such structures keep out gulls, foxes, and raccoons, they also attract the attention of these animals; in the time it takes for a predator to explore the boundaries of the exclosure and decide that he can't get in, adult plovers will sometimes abandon the nest. Furthermore, exclosures reduce predation on eggs, but not on hatchlings, which quickly leave the nest area and disperse widely outside the fence. In an effort to reduce predation, park staff routinely trap and remove or kill foxes and raccoons. However, it has proven impossible to trap all the predators on Assateague, and they still affect piping plover populations.

Piping plovers will likely never become common enough to no longer require regulatory protection. Their nesting habitat on open beaches ensures that piping plover reproductive success will never be high. Expect that the forebeach, dunes, and washover flats at Assateague will remain off limits to hikers each spring. But this minor inconvenience is a small price to pay for the assurance that piping plovers, and the full biological diversity of this wild barrier island, will be a part of the Assateague experience for decades and generations to come.

Nassawango Creek Preserve: Paul Leifer Trail and Furnace Town

County: Worcester

Distance: About 1 mile; circuit hike

Difficulty: Easy. Flat; sandy to muddy terrain

Dogs: Prohibited

Why It's Special: A historic restored village providing dryshod foot access to a beautiful, diverse bald cypress swamp

More Information: Furnace Town, www.furnacetown.org, (410) 632-2032; The Nature Conservancy (Maryland), (301) 897-8570

Street Address: 3816 Old Furnace Road, Snow Hill, Maryland 21863

GPS Coordinates: 38.203207, 75.470161 (Furnace Town Visitor Center)

The cypress swamps of the Pocomoke River watershed are best explored by canoe, but for those who want to visit this unique habitat on foot, the Nature Conservancy has established the Paul Leifer Nature Trail. This woodchip and boardwalk path leads through the forest along the edge of Nassawango Creek, a major tributary of the Pocomoke. The trail is adjacent to Furnace Town, a partially restored iron smelter village dating from the early 1800s. Exhibits at Furnace Town portray daily life in this now remote but once busy and well-populated corner of Maryland.

Because of the difficulty of cutting trail through the boggy soil and tangled growth of swamps like this one, and the desire to disturb the swamp to the smallest extent possible, the Paul Leifer Trail is only about a mile in length. It is flat but can have puddles and muddy spots. Birdwatchers and wildflower lovers will want to go slowly, however, especially in late spring when flora and fauna are at their peak diversity. Combined with a tour of Furnace Town, the trail described here makes an easy half-day exploration.

Trip Description

Access to the Paul Leifer Trail is across the property of Furnace Town. The nonprofit group operating and restoring the village asks you to register with them first, and an admission fee is charged. A small museum documenting life at the iron furnace is next door. Several other interesting exhibits are scattered about the property in separate buildings. Restrooms, water, picnic tables, trash cans, and a soda machine are available here.

From the museum, walk toward the remains of the iron furnace. Made of brick, it is thirty-five feet high and twenty-four feet square at the base. Hot blast tubes at the top were a later addition meant to increase the efficiency of burning. The furnace was loaded with a layer of charcoal, then a layer of bog iron, then oyster shells as a flux. This layering was repeated many times. A bellows run by a waterwheel provided oxygen to the mixture. When fired, the melted bog ore was let out at the casting hearth, the oyster shells removing impurities. Between 1828 and 1850, the iron furnace produced about 700 tons of pig iron annually.

The source of ore for the furnace was a peculiar complex of iron found in certain coastal plain streams and known as bog iron. As rainwater filters through the decaying vegetable matter of bogs, it assumes greater acidity. This acid water dissolves iron in the soil, which emerges as bluish slicks on the surface of still water and in complex with sand as bog iron. This was the source of much of the iron smelted in the colonies and in the United States until about 1850, when purer sources of iron ore became available.

Begin at a bulletin board in back of the smelter. The trail is roughly in the shape of a figure eight; casual visitors generally prefer the shorter circuit. The first portion of the trail runs along the edge of the swamp. To the left, the land is about a foot lower in elevation, putting it in the floodplain of Nassawango Creek. The black, mucky soil, rich in organic matter, is also relatively poor in oxygen. For this reason, anaerobic bacteria lend the characteristic "rotten egg" smell associated with wet areas.

The hydric soil conditions limit the kinds of plants that can grow

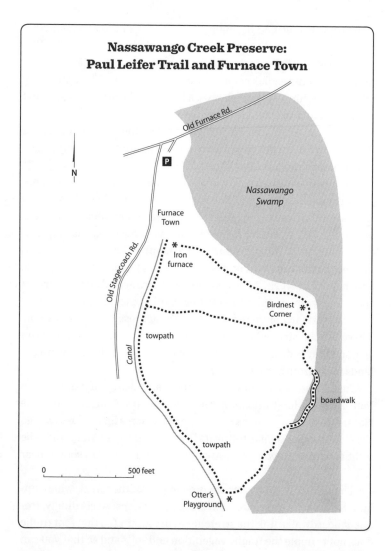

Nassawango Creek Preserve:
Paul Leifer Trail and Furnace Town

there; almost all of them are specific to wetlands. Look for sphagnum moss lying directly on the substrate. Although it is not as deep or as widespread here as in a true bog like Cranesville in western Maryland, sphagnum is present on these permanently muddy soils. Its foliage was used to dress wounds during the Civil War because bacteria could not live in the acidic water trapped among the leaves. The bright red spike of the cardinal flower decorates these wetlands in late summer. Cinnamon ferns are very common here—large, graceful ferns easily identified by "hairy armpits": the base of each leaflet where it joins the stalk has a tuft of brown "hairs."

The wetland forest is dominated by bald cypress, coniferous trees that shed their needles each autumn. They are easily identified by their stringy, fibrous, reddish brown bark and the many "knees" that often surround the trunks. Other trees in the swamp include sweetgum and holly on higher sites and the ubiquitous red maple. These forests have been cut repeatedly since colonial times, supplying charcoal for the operation of the furnace.

At the first sharp turn, known as Birdnest Corner, look for woodpeckers and, in spring, prothonotary warblers nesting in cavities in several swamp trees. The latter, with bright yellow chests and heads and bluish wings, are both spectacular and engaging, chasing each other in territorial displays during the month of May. Prothonotaries may be the defining bird of wooded swamps in southern Maryland, and they are a favorite of birdwatchers everywhere. At least fourteen species of warblers raise their young in this dense swamp.

Just a bit farther up the trail, look for depressions in the swamp. These are the sites where bog ore was mined more than 150 years ago, and they indicate the slow rate of the recovery that some fragile lands make from human insults.

Just ahead are a trail junction and a sign dedicating the path to Paul Leifer, a longtime member of the Nature Conservancy. The Nature Conservancy owns more than 9,000 acres in the Nassawango Creek watershed, constituting its largest property in Maryland. The right fork returns you promptly to Furnace Town. You should bear left.

The trail now enters a more broken part of the forest, where upland hammocks alternate with wetland swamps. Accordingly, frequent boardwalks link the stretches of dry ground so that foot traffic does not trample the fragile vegetation and soils and so that you can view the swamp closely and with dry feet.

After at least a half mile, the trail reaches its deepest penetration into the woods. Ahead the trail turns right to parallel the remains of an old canal. This canal allowed pig iron to be floated from the furnace to Nassawango Creek and thence down the Pocomoke to distant ports. This point is known as the Otter's Playground; in winter, river otters slide down the bank into the icy water over and over again.

Iron furnace

The trail runs straight now, directly back to the furnace, on a berm of soil excavated when the canal was built. This upland section of the forest is a habitat distinct from the wetland swamp forest. It is dominated by loblolly pine; water, red, and white oak; holly; sweetgum; and dogwood. Among the more unusual flora, look for muscadine grape vines twining over branches and with stringlike aerial roots. Like many other life forms inhabiting the Nassawango watershed, they are at the northern edge of their distribution here. Greenbrier and poison ivy are other common vines that make trailblazing difficult in these areas. In May, pink lady's slipper orchids brighten the forest floor, especially under pine trees. Indeed, fifteen species of orchids have been counted in the Pocomoke River watershed.

After about a mile, the trail returns to the furnace area, where your walk is concluded.

Directions

From Baltimore or Washington, take Route 50 across the Bay Bridge to Salisbury. In the downtown area, turn right on Route 12. After about 15 miles, turn right on Old Furnace Road, where there is a sign for Furnace Town. Proceed about a mile to the park entrance. Furnace Town is open daily from 11 a.m. to 5 p.m. Access to the Paul Leifer Trail coincides with Furnace Town's hours of operation.

Other Outdoor Recreational Opportunities Nearby

Canoe/kayak access to Nassawango Creek is just a mile or so away, and the creek is a beautiful place to paddle. The Pocomoke River and Corkers Creek are just a bit farther away. Canoes and kayaks for all three creeks may be rented in Snow Hill, Maryland, from the Pocomoke River Canoe Company, www.pocomokeriverpaddle.com.

WHY SAVE ENDANGERED SPECIES?

Since the passage of the Endangered Species Act by the US Congress in 1972, the general public has expressed great interest in rare and unusual organisms. This has been especially true of large, beautiful animals ("charismatic megafauna") like wolves and eagles. The immense majority of species considered endangered, however, are neither big nor especially attractive, and most are not even animals. For example, Maryland, which has assembled its own list of rare, endangered, and threatened species within the state, listed 167 animals and 445 plants as of 2016. Few naturalists have even heard of, let alone seen, such unusual animals as the green floater (a mollusc), Walker's tusked sprawler (an insect), the Cheat minnow (a fish), or the southern pygmy shrew (a mammal). The plants are even more obscure: twining bartonia, shaved sedge, anglepod, floating paspalum, and a host of others. Fungi, bacteria, and algae have never been investigated, let alone listed.

Why this interest in such obscure organisms? Three general reasons for preserving endangered species have been put forth.

First, such species may have an important use to humankind at some point in the future. In medical science, plant extracts are sometimes helpful in therapies. In addition to being a source of drugs, plants are our primary source of food. Modern food plants are highly inbred strains whose ancestors and close relatives should be preserved as a source of genetic diversity for breeding in specialized traits that might be required in the future. Animals can also be of value. For example, the armadillo (although not endangered) is the best experimental model for the study of leprosy. In essence, preservation of all species ensures more options for the future.

Second, endangered species are biological indicators of the health of the ecological community in which they reside. Most species are endangered because of the action or activity of humans in that community, whether it be loss of habitat via human modification, pollution, or the introduction of non-native species. As bioindicators, they report to us on the status of the natural world and what effect our activities have.

Third, rare species should be conserved for aesthetic reasons. Even though they are obscure, many of these organisms enrich our appreciation and enjoyment of the natural world. They may have no economic value, but they are nonetheless valuable.

Finally, as the dominant life form on our planet today, humans have a moral responsibility to other organisms. Extinctions are a commonplace occurrence in the natural world, but the pace of extinctions is far greater now than at any time in the past. The only reason for this high rate of extinction is our own short-sighted and careless attitude toward other living things.

These are all altruistic reasons, good for humankind as a group as well as for the organisms in question. But individuals

(continued)

may not be able or willing to practice such altruistic behavior. For example, developers who are prevented from building on a piece of land because it harbors an endangered species invariably feel that an exception should be made and development allowed, or that they should be duly compensated by society. The controversy over the spotted owl in the forests of the Pacific Northwest is a case in point.

In the past, concern for endangered species has led to a never-ending sequence of crises to be dealt with rather than a farsighted, carefully planned strategy for preservation. In addition, management by crisis has been expensive in terms of time, personnel, and money (especially legal fees). Most recovery programs deal with showy or charismatic species, but these are merely the most obvious representatives of a cast that includes thousands of supporting players that make up the foundation of the ecological community. Scientists and environmental activists believe that conservation now must go beyond merely a concern for species that are rare. Emphasis should now be placed on conservation of biological diversity, on the entire range of organisms in the context of their environment. The advantage of such an approach lies in its flexibility, timeliness, and cost effectiveness. If critical habitats and hotspots of biodiversity can be identified and preserved, other less critical parts of the landscape will be available for human activities.

Pickering Creek
Audubon Center

County: Talbot

Distance: 2.9 miles as described; circuit hike

Difficulty: Easy. Flat; sometimes muddy

Dogs: Prohibited on trails

Why It's Special: An excellent environmental education sanctuary featuring a coastal plain old growth forest, waterfowl, tidewater views, and small boat access

More Information: Pickering Creek Audubon Center, www.pickeringcreek.org, (410) 822-4903

Street Address: 11450 Audubon Lane, Easton, Maryland 21601

GPS Coordinates: 38.859927, 76.123924 (trailhead)

Tucked away among the soybean fields of rural Talbot County is a wonderful place of wetland ponds bursting with life, a rare coastal plain old growth forest where oaks, beeches, and pines tower overhead and where views of the Chesapeake tidewater invite quiet contemplation. Although not well known outside the mid-Shore community, Pickering Creek packs several diverse habitats in close proximity, and a visit makes for a rewarding day of hiking, nature study, and even paddling. Pickering has an active environmental education program that serves more than 13,000 students of all ages annually, but the property never feels crowded. Best of all, the trails are open 365 days a year, dawn to dusk, free of charge.

Trip Description

Upon arrival at Pickering Creek, park near the Welcome Center and its attendant sheds. There is a portable restroom here but no water. After registering, walk across the dusty parking area to a sign board marking the entrance to the Wetlands Overlook Trail. The initial few hundred yards pass through an old agricultural field left fallow since about 2005 and now grown up in grasses, shrubs, and young trees. The dense vegetation is home to a wide variety of insects and spiders, who in turn are prey for the sparrows, quail, meadowlarks, and other birds that like this thick cover.

In March, woodcocks use this area as their lekking grounds. As dusk descends, males launch themselves from the ground, climbing to as much as several hundred feet in the air. Then they drop downward, wind whistling through their wings, their twittering calls echoing in the gloaming, as they display for females on the ground below. This nightly mating ritual is one of the wonders of the animal world and is not to be missed. Pickering Creek offers guided woodcock walks annually.

At the first turn, a deck looks out over a pond that is bordered by wetland vegetation. At dusk in springtime, a variety of amphibians sing their choruses here. Wood, pickerel, leopard, and chorus frogs, as well as spring peepers, are commonly heard. You may be surprised to discover that all these amphibians arrived here only since 2005, when the ponds were created , proving the "field of dreams" hypothesis that if you build it, they will come.

Another quarter mile leads to a large observation platform overlooking another set of ponds. In winter, Canada geese and a variety of ducks are commonly seen. In spring, wood ducks raise broods of young here, and red-winged blackbirds quarrel among the cattails and other wetland vegetation.

The trail continues along the edge of this field, and after two more turns reaches the vicinity of the parking area. Assuming you wish to continue walking and visit some new habitats, turn left on the Pond Loop Trail. This small impoundment is surrounded by bald cypress, an unusual tree to be found this far north on the Eastern Shore. Kingfishers, great blue herons, and wood ducks are often seen here. At the dam end of the pond, turn left again onto the Farm to Bay Loop Trail.

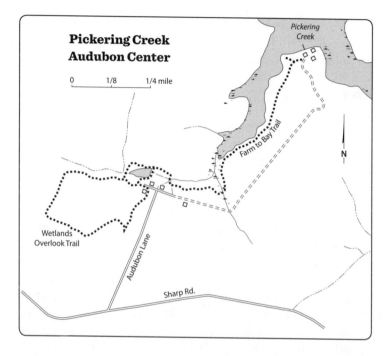

After crossing the little stream at the head of an arm of Pickering Creek, you will encounter a small wooden house just off the trail. Take a moment to visit the reconstructed home of Gilbert Byron, a poet and author who lived in this tiny house for many decades. His memoir of his boyhood in rural Talbot County in the early 1900s, *The Lord's Oysters,* is a fond and poignant story of a simpler time. The house was moved to Pickering Creek when its original location was sold, and it has been lovingly restored only to the extent necessary. It's an interesting paean to Byron's Thoreauvian existence.

While you are detouring, take some time to study the Children's Imagination Garden, just across the lane. Here you will find a well-tended set of both wild and cultivated plant species used in environmental education programs at the Center.

Return to the Farm to Bay Trail, which runs through a narrow buffer strip of forest within view of the tidal Pickering Creek. After a quarter mile or so, the forest becomes more expansive. This forty-acre parcel is a mature forest that has not been disturbed in well over a century, and it is slowly taking on characteristics of an old growth forest. Huge beeches and oaks cast a dense shade on the forest floor, and there is little undergrowth. Such habitat is home to the Delmarva fox squirrel, a mammal that was uncommon when Pickering Creek first became a sanctuary in the early 1980s. Since then, Delmarvas have expanded greatly across the Eastern Shore, reaching more than 20,000 individuals in ten counties. Once on the federal endangered species list, Delmarva fox squirrels have increased their numbers to the point where the population is now considered recovered, and the species was removed from the list in 2015. Delmarvas are about twice as large as the familiar gray squirrel, have lighter colored fur, larger ears, and have the habit of dashing across the forest floor when disturbed, rather than climbing the nearest tree.

As you walk, take time to enjoy this rare coastal plain mature forest. Wood thrushes, a species of concern to the National Audubon Society because its numbers have been declining, sings its beautiful flutelike song here in late spring. Owls, both barred and great horned, hoot in the gloaming. Mountain laurels bloom in May, their white flowers almost ghostlike in the deep shade. The many mature American beech trees host a parasitic plant, beech drops, at great density. Beech drops do not contain chlorophyll and do not perform photosynthesis, instead obtaining nutrients from the roots of beech trees. Their pale yellow stalks are conspicuous on the forest floor and persist throughout the winter.

The trail ends at the waterfront activity center. There are wonderful views of Pickering Creek from the picnic tables; Wye Island is in the distance. In fall and winter, Canada geese spend each night on the creek, their calls echoing across the water. In late afternoon, vultures circle overhead in what are called "advertising flights," signaling to their cohorts where they plan to spend the night. Bald eagles are occasional visitors to the creek as well. The main house contains offices, a library, and some displays; when staff is present, you may rent a canoe or kayak. (If you have your own boat, you may drive to this point and launch without charge, as long as there are no other events going on.)

To complete the hiking circuit, return to your car on the mile-long dirt road that runs between the waterfront and the Welcome Center where you parked. With forest on one side and agricultural fields on the other, there is always something new and interesting to see on the return trip.

Photo courtesy of Pickering Creek Audubon Center

Directions

From Washington or Baltimore, cross the Chesapeake Bay on Route 50. From where the Bay Bridge enters Kent Island, proceed 20 miles on Route 50. Turn right on Route 662 at mile marker 58, just beyond Skipton Creek. (Note: Route 662 intersects Route 50 at several places, so it's important to note both mileage and these landmarks.) Once on Route 662, go 1.9 miles. Turn right on Sharp Road and go 1.5 miles. Turn right onto the continuation of Sharp Road (there is a sign for "Sharp Road to Presquile Road"). Go 1.4 miles to the entrance to Pickering Creek Audubon Center, which is marked by a sign.

Other Outdoor Recreational Opportunities Nearby

There is nothing else close, but Tuckahoe State Park, with hiking and paddling trails, is located about a thirty-minute drive away. Blackwater National Wildlife Refuge, with cycling and paddling venues, is about a forty-five-minute drive from Pickering Creek.

JELLYFISH

Chesapeake Bay is the most prominent geological feature of Maryland, bisecting the state from south to north. It is greatly loved by citizens, but its waters have one major drawback: a significant amount of the Chesapeake is unswimmable in the summer and early fall. This remarkable misfortune is due to the ubiquitous presence of *Chrysaora quinquecirrha*, the stinging sea nettle. These jellyfish sting immediately upon even a brushing contact, producing a painful, fiery, itching rash that persists for twenty minutes or so. Neither big nor fierce, jellyfish are nevertheless among the most feared animals in Maryland.

What the jellyfish lacks in size it makes up for in numbers. Stand on a dock in mid-Bay in August and it seems that every square foot of water has its own jellyfish, pulsing and throbbing in mindless menace. Yet jellyfish are not present every year; their spread is highly dependent on salinity. In wet years, when freshwater inflow from the Susquehanna and other tributaries measurably dilutes salty water from the ocean, jellyfish stay in the saline waters of the lower Bay. Even in dry years, beaches of the northern Bay are usually free of sea nettles.

Sea nettles are rather simple organisms, but the cells that sting, called nematocysts, are fairly sophisticated. Thousands of these cells coat each tentacle. Each nematocyst has a trigger attached to a capsule, inside of which the stinging filament is coiled. When the trigger brushes against something, it opens the capsule's trapdoor and the coiled stinging filament is propelled outward. The filament is coated with venom and is also barbed so that the venom will remain in contact with the victim. The result is pure pain. Should you be so unfortunate as to be stung, prompt application of meat tenderizer (which degrades the venom) may be helpful.

Sea nettles have a complex life cycle of which most people are unaware. Adult male jellyfish release sperm into the water; females pump that water past their eggs and fertilization occurs. Tiny larvae called planulae develop; these are released to float freely with the other plankton of Chesapeake Bay. After a short time, the planulae settle to the bottom and attach to a solid substrate much as do oyster and barnacle larvae. They soon develop into the polyp stage, tiny vaselike structures. Polyps overwinter in this portion of their life cycle, forming cysts if the weather gets too cold or if they are subjected to other environmental insults. In spring, the polyps begin to grow again and mature to bud off a floating stage. Called ephyra, these tiny discs resume a planktonic existence. They eventually grow tentacles and begin to look like mature jellyfish.

Adult jellyfish are free-floating, although they can propel themselves with contractions of the body. They feed on small fish and other animals that they encounter, immobilizing the prey by stinging. The prey is then taken into the transparent bell, where digestion occurs. Having evolved more than 250 million years ago and thrived in estuarine waters ever since, sea nettles are eminently successful, well-adapted creatures. If only they weren't such a pain.

Tuckahoe State Park
and Adkins Arboretum

Counties: Queen Anne's, Caroline

Distance: 7.8 miles as described; circuit hike

Difficulty: Easy. Mostly flat with a few short hills; sandy terrain

Dogs: Permitted on leash

Why It's Special: A beautiful Eastern Shore riparian forest and a fine arboretum known for birds, orchids, and other plants

More Information: Tuckahoe State Park, http://dnr.maryland.gov /publiclands/pages/eastern/tuckahoe.aspx, (410) 820-1668; Adkins Arboretum, http://adkinsarboretum.org, (410) 634-2847

Street Address: Trailhead: near 13122 Crouse Mill Road, Ridgely, Maryland, 21660; Adkins Arboretum: 12610 Eveland Road, Ridgely, Maryland, 21660

GPS Coordinates: 38.966393, 75.939470 (trailhead)

Any discussion of plants growing in the counties of Maryland's mid–Eastern Shore would feature the state's Big Three: corn, soybeans, and winter wheat. That reflects the farming heritage of Queen Anne's, Talbot, Kent, and Caroline Counties. But native plants like springtime ephemeral forest wildflowers? Where would they grow amid those tens of thousands of acres of farm fields that stretch to the horizon? That such a place exists makes it all the more valuable and unique. Tuckahoe State Park encompasses almost 4,000 acres of maturing forest on both sides of Tuckahoe Creek. And in the heart of Tuckahoe is Adkins Arboretum, a private, nonprofit organization dedicated to conservation of and education about plants of the Delmarva peninsula. Adkins has an extensive trail network in its 400 acres, and these trails are an intrinsic part

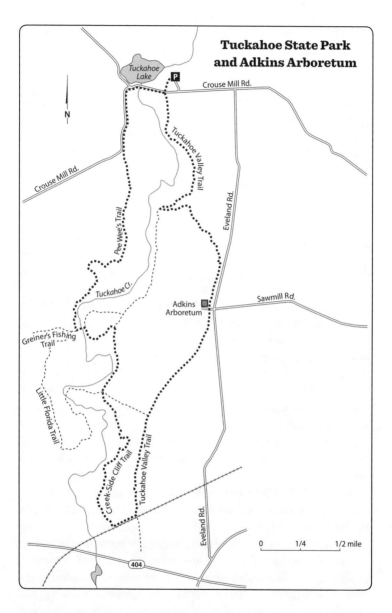

**Tuckahoe State Park
and Adkins Arboretum**

of the larger trail system of Tuckahoe State Park. A walk here gives
the hiker a new appreciation of the wonders of the Coastal Plain,
that flat land of sandy and gravelly soils that makes up most of the
Eastern Shore of Maryland.

The route described below combines many but not all the trails of Tuckahoe, and just one of several at Adkins. Taken together, they pass through virtually all the habitats of the mid-Shore: riparian and upland forest and land in various stages of succession, from abandoned farm fields to shrubby grasslands to sapling-stage woods. This is a fine venue for birding, with so many habitats in close association; indeed, the area has been deemed an Important Bird Area by the National Audubon Society. Finally, this may be the Delmarva's best location for native orchids, especially pink lady's slippers in late spring, and cranefly orchid, modest at the flowering stage but with conspicuous leaves in fall and winter.

Trip Description

A convenient place to begin your hike is from the picnic area parking lot of Tuckahoe State Park, just off Crouse Mill Road and only a few yards from Tuckahoe Lake. There are restrooms and drinking water here, and shade is provided by the tall loblolly pines towering over the picnic area. The park rents canoes and kayaks from the lake beach from April until October.

From the picnic area, walk west along the broad grassy shoulders of Crouse Mill Road, with the millpond on your right. Cross over Tuckahoe Creek and bear left at the road intersection (still Crouse Mill Road). Although this first half mile is inauspicious, being just a road shoulder, things will soon improve. Leave the road and enter the forest at the well-marked sign for the Pee Wee's Trail, blazed in orange.

Pee Wee's Trail is often used by horses and their riders, since the Tuckahoe Equestrian Center is immediately across the street from the trailhead and Pee Wee's is the only way to easily access the rest of the trails in Tuckahoe from this point. Since horse hooves disturb the soil, poison ivy grows copiously along the edges of the trail as upright woody plants with leaves in leaflets of three. (Poison ivy also grows as a hairy vine on tree trunks.) Another common woody plant here is pawpaw, a shrub or small tree up to a dozen feet in height with large, oblong leaves tapering to a fine point. Mature pawpaws have tasty fruits in early September, but these trees are all (unfortunately) immature. The trail follows a winding path, reaching the edge of Tuckahoe Creek twice and at other times following a side stream uphill until an easy crossing point is achieved. After one mile in the forest, the trail opens into a grassy area along the creek, where there is a sturdy footbridge across the Tuckahoe. This is a popular fishing hole.

Cross over the bridge and turn right on the blue-blazed Tuckahoe Valley Trail. After just a quarter mile, bear right, still on the Tuckahoe Valley Trail. Another half mile of pleasant walking brings you to a major trail intersection. The Turkey Hill Trail, on your right, merely goes down to the river and an equestrian crossing site that is too deep for hikers even in dry weather. To your left, the Tuckahoe Valley Trail follows an old road toward private farmland. Instead, go straight on the yellow-blazed Creekside Cliff Trail.

This is a fairly narrow foot trail that changes direction frequently and even has some small elevation changes. True to its name, parts of the Creekside Cliff Trail run along the top edge of a steep hillside, where there are nice views of the Tuckahoe floodplain about 40 feet below. American beech trees are common here, their handsome smooth gray bark unmarred in this remote location by the penknife-etched graffiti so typically inscribed on this species. After a mile of such pleasant walking, you will emerge from the trees and pass under a power line. In another 50 feet, turn left on an old railbed, recognizable by the packed gravel underfoot.

This is the site of the long-abandoned Chesapeake Railroad that once ran from Easton, Maryland, to Clayton, Delaware, servicing the farms, grain elevators, and agricultural supply houses of central Delmarva. At some point in the future, a multiuse trail may be developed along this route.

In a few hundred yards the railbed becomes overgrown, and no further progress along it is possible. To your right is a cemetery; it is private property. Turn left, cross a footbridge, and the route now becomes a wide multiuse trail surfaced in crushed limestone. Constructed in 2016, this trail is, for now, part of the Tuckahoe Valley Trail. It winds its way in picturesque curves through a young forest of no particular distinction, passing over several well-constructed bridges. After one mile, the blue-blazed Tuckahoe Valley Trail branches off to the left; stay with the multiuse path.

The remainder of this 2.5-mile multi-use trail has no name as of this writing (2017). Continue along it, past agricultural fields; the path eventually converges with Eveland Road. Pass by the driveway to the Tuckahoe State Park office and then turn into the next driveway at the sign for the Adkins Arboretum plant nursery.

The land that now forms Adkins Arboretum was once reserved for a Maryland state arboretum. Public funding was scarce, however, and in 1998, the ambitious and better-funded Friends of Adkins Arboretum proposed a public/private partnership to the state. A fifty-year lease was put in place, and the Arboretum is now run as a private, nonprofit organization. There is a fine Visitor Center, trails are open to the public daily, educational activities for schoolchildren and the general public are held, and botanical research is conducted. A network of foot trails (also open to equestrians and cyclists) weaves through the 400 acres. These trails are well marked with modern signage, and many species of plants are identified.

Just after entering the arboretum, turn right on a gravel road, which soon passes the Visitor Center. Just beyond this point, enter the forest on a trail marked "Woodland walks." In the next few hundred yards, the exceptional nature of this area becomes apparent. In May, pink lady's slipper orchids dot the woods, blooming in an attractive fashion. These are large flowers, with the "slipper" more than a cubic inch in volume. Deep pink veins create a filamentous pattern on the outer edge of the bright pink slipper.

Even more common are cranefly orchids. In autumn and winter, a green leaf lying just above the duff of the forest floor is conspicuous. The underside of the leaf is bright magenta, while the top of the leaf is dark green studded with brown, raised bumps. By the time the forest leafs out in late April, these leaves are gone. Then, in July and August, cranefly orchids flower. A series of dull-colored flowers line a stem less than two feet high. Unlike the flowers of many other orchids, cranefly orchid is not conspicuous at all. They are pollinated by night-flying moths, so color is irrelevant. A keen observer will see hundreds of cranefly orchid leaves on a late autumn walk at Adkins, and indeed throughout Tuckahoe State Park.

As a footbridge comes into sight, turn right on the blue-blazed Tuckahoe Valley Trail, labeled "north" on the sign. From this point, it's about a mile of pleasant woodland hiking to the trailhead at Crouse Mill Road.

Directions

From either Baltimore or Washington, DC, cross the Chesapeake Bay Bridge on Route 50. At Route 404, turn left. Go 6.8 miles. Turn left at Ridgely Road, at a stoplight. Go 100 yards and turn left on Eveland Road. Go to the end and turn left on Crouse Mill Road. Within 200 yards, turn right into a driveway that leads to the picnic area. Alternatively, there is plenty of roadside parking just ahead on Crouse Mill Road.

Other Outdoor Recreational Opportunities Nearby

Tuckahoe State Park rents canoes and kayaks at the lake in warmer weather; it's possible to paddle upstream almost two miles through a lovely swamp and riparian forest that always has lots of wildlife.

LADY'S SLIPPER ORCHIDS

Among the most sought-after and admired species that compose Maryland's natural heritage are several kinds of wild orchids. Although none is common and several are on the rare, endangered, or threatened list, pink lady's slipper and yellow lady's slipper are occasionally found by alert hikers. These slipper orchids are so named because their flower resembles a shoe; other common names include moccasin flower or, even more charmingly, whippoorwill's shoe. Both pink and yellow lady's slippers are woodland wildflowers. The pink variety prefers drier and more acidic soil and may be a bit more common on the Coastal Plain in pine forests. The yellow is more typical of Piedmont forests with rich, deep, complex soils.

Orchids are uncommon in Maryland because of habitat loss and overharvesting. Conversion of mature forest into land for agriculture, development, and timber harvesting wipes out populations of woodland orchids. Indeed, the journals of naturalists in the eighteenth and early nineteenth centuries make it clear that orchids were common plants in then-undisturbed forests. Among

(continued)

those orchid colonies that have survived, collection by gardeners and commercial suppliers also takes a toll. This is unfortunate, because lady's slipper orchids never transplant successfully. Similarly, they cannot be grown from seed or by dividing rhizomes; most lady's slippers offered for sale have merely been dug up from a wild population.

Lady's slipper orchids are tightly adapted to their habitat. Specific conditions of microclimate, soil nutrient balance, soil pH, and microbial flora are required. A germinated seed does not emerge from its seed coat until the next year and usually takes three years to develop its first leaves. During this time, the embryo is nourished by specific strains of soil fungi. The fungal threads, or hyphae, invade the plant through a root tip and penetrate through several layers of cells to the cortex. The plant then extracts water and sugars from the fungus. Although most such mycorrhizal interactions are mutually beneficial, science has yet to learn what benefit the fungus derives from the orchid in this case. The plant-fungus relationship continues throughout the life span of the plant, which may be considerable; an orchid can take up to ten years to produce its first flower, and it will then continue flowering for many more seasons.

Yellow lady's slippers tend to be found in colonies. Some colonies are actually only a single individual plant, a complex net of rhizomes and roots studded with occasional above-ground shoots. This configuration explains the confusion of the great American botanist Asa Gray, who could not understand why colonies of yellow lady's slippers produced so few seeds.

The flower structure of lady's slipper orchids has evolved to ensure pollination. The most common pollinators are bumblebees, which enter the flower by the large opening. Because the sides of the slipper are recurved, the bumblebee cannot climb back out. Instead, she eventually finds one of two smaller holes near the heel of the slipper. As she leaves, pollen packets clinging to her back are scraped off by barbs on the stigma of the flower, located just above the opening. A bit farther along, a stamen deposits a sticky pollen packet on the bee to transport to the next orchid. These specific interactions between orchid flowers and their pollinating insects were the topic of an entire (but obscure) book by Charles Darwin, written in 1862 to support his theory of natural selection.

There is little that can be done to conserve Maryland's wild orchids except to leave them alone. Some wildflower enthusiasts will tell only their most trusted friends where a colony is located. Never pick or dig up an orchid! In addition, since orchids tend to be found in older forests, as much acreage as possible should be kept undisturbed to preserve suitable habitat.

Calvert Cliffs State Park

County: Calvert

Distance: 4.3 miles as described; circuit hike

Difficulty: Easy. Mostly flat with a few small rises; sandy terrain

Dogs: Permitted on leash

Why It's Special: A lovely walk through a coastal plain forest leading to views of Calvert Cliffs; the opportunity to sort through tidal gravels in search of Miocene fossils

More Information: Calvert Cliffs State Park, c/o Smallwood State Park, http://dnr.maryland.gov/publiclands/Pages/southern/calvertcliffs.aspx, (301) 743-7613

Street Address: 10540 H.G. Trueman Road, Lusby, Maryland 20657

GPS Coordinates: 38.394102, 76.435819 (trailhead)

The state of Maryland has many natural resources within its boundaries, but perhaps none is more famous (and justifiably so) than the paleontological site at Calvert Cliffs. For at least the last 150 years, fossils of scientific import have been extracted from the cliffs and have been studied at facilities as prestigious as the Smithsonian Institution. In addition, generations of young students have had their interest piqued and imaginations excited by the treasure trove of fossilized shark teeth found in the wave-washed gravel at the base of the cliffs.

The cliffs containing the fossil-bearing strata stretch almost thirty miles, from Fairhaven to Drum Point. Most of the coast is privately owned, and public access to the cliffs is not possible without the specific permission of the landowners. Only at a few places, like Calvert Cliffs State Park, can the public view the sandy bluffs. Unfortunately, the threat of excavation of the cliffs by visitors and the resultant increased rate of erosion, as well as the danger of cliff

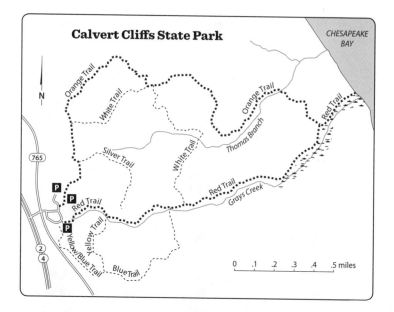

collapse, has caused the Department of Natural Resources to prohibit public access to the cliffs and adjacent shoreline. What remains for the visitor to the bayfront is a short, narrow stretch of beach about 100 yards long where you can pan the intertidal gravel for fossils or view the cliffs.

There are several trails winding through Calvert Cliffs State Park, but the most direct route to the water is on the Red Trail. Fortunately, it is also a very scenic one, winding through a beautiful Coastal Plain forest rich with ferns and bird life. As such, it makes a nice destination for a family hike, a morning birdwalk, or an afternoon of botanizing. The return trip, on the Orange Trail, takes a more circuitous route through a designated Wildlands that has large trees, hilly terrain, and a remote, untrammeled feel. The walk described totals 4.3 miles round trip.

Trip Description

Calvert Cliffs is a small park, and its developed area, just a few yards off Route 4, occupies only two or three acres. There are parking places for more than a hundred cars, wheelchair-accessible bathrooms, a number of picnic tables, and a large playground for children.

A small fishing pond is adjacent to the parking lot, and it is popular with local kids. All hiking trails depart from this area.

The most direct trail to the bayfront is the Red Trail, denoted by waist-high posts every 0.1 miles. Running alongside a small stream, Grays Creek, for its entire length, it is also the most interesting trail in terms of scenic beauty and wildlife. Leaving the parking lot at the uphill side of the pond, it skirts the water's edge, where croaking frogs can be heard and turtles and dragonflies seen. The trail then enters the woods. Although the trail has only slight dips and rises, the many roots crossing its path make for uneven footing. Also striking is the hilly nature of the land, unusual for a site in the coastal plain near the Bay. Although the hills are small (less than fifty feet in height), they give the land a dissected feel that also creates varying micro-habitats, depending on the direction the hillside faces, its degree of shading, and its nearness to surface water.

As might be expected, the soil is a fine white sand enriched by organic matter only near the surface. Some parts of the trail are in-cised into the hill, and these exposures are a good place to examine the various layers of soil. Sandy soils are considered dry soils; if you were to pour a bucket of water onto sand, it would rapidly percolate through, draining from the interstices between the tiny, rock-hard grains. Thus, even in a well-watered climate, sandy soils are xeric in nature and support only those plant species that can exist in water- and nutrient-poor soil. For this reason, mountain laurel and American holly are very common; there may be more of these two small trees here than along any other trail in Maryland. Several kinds of oaks, hickories, loblolly pines, and Virginia pines are also common trees. Drought-tolerant mosses hug the ground and help retain moisture for tiny insects and other forest floor inhabitants.

Because the trail follows the stream, however, water is more accessible to species living in its floodplain, and that available soil water helps to diversify the flora. Sweet gum, tulip poplar, American beech, and red maple are all commonly found here. Many specimens are quite tall, and the straight trunks and lack of low branches on tulip poplar and sweet gum trees give the forest an open feel. Cinnamon ferns, Christmas ferns, and interrupted ferns dot the forest floor near the stream.

After about three-quarters of a mile, the stream spreads out and meanders into a swamp. An earthen berm occupies the far end of the little valley, backing up the waters into an artificial nontidal wetland. Many of the trees in the swamp appear to be doing poorly and seem to be dead except for a few branches of green leaves. Virtually every tree in this swamp is green ash, a hardy, water-tolerant tree that assumes this style of growth under hydric conditions. Note that not a single green ash can be found anywhere else in the forest; it is unable to compete with other species on upland, well-drained sites. The many dead snags make fine perches for birds like osprey, hawks, kingfishers, and herons, and birdwatching here can be rewarding, especially in the spring. Closer to the berm, the wetland is wider and has fewer trees still standing; arrow arum dominates this freshwater marsh. It is easily recognized by its large, triangular-shaped leaves that give it a tropical look. In late summer, the black seeds fall onto the muddy substrate, where they are eaten by wood ducks; hence this plant's other common name, "duck corn."

If you're observant, you'll note a beaver lodge near the middle of the swamp. These beavers often add sticks and branches to the water outlet in the berm in an effort to raise water levels in the swamp. Park staff clear these branches periodically, managing the swamp not just for beaver but also for wood duck, who prefer a lower, muckier water level.

The Red Trail is heavily used, and volunteers have laid boardwalks in places where the trail is muddy. They have also constructed a series of wooden benches, each with a rain canopy, at strategic rest stops or scenic views. Calvert Cliffs State Park has an active "Friends of" group, and they have done a first-rate job of making this trail user friendly.

Within 200 yards of the berm, you arrive at Chesapeake Bay. There are fine views of the Calvert Cliffs to both the north and the south, although access to the base of the cliffs is blocked by hurricane fences. The cliffs undergo continual erosion, especially during winter storms, and can be dangerous where undercut. They are home to one of Maryland's endangered species, the puritan tiger beetle. This little beetle, less than an inch long, is known from about ten sites in Calvert County and from one other site along the Connecticut River. Its larval stage lives in the cliffs; when adults emerge to mate in early summer, they use the narrow stretches of nearby beach.

The gravel intertidal at the Calvert Cliffs can be a good place to look for fossil shark teeth, especially after a storm event that erodes

the cliffs. The occasional three-inch great white shark tooth is found, but the smaller teeth are by far the most common. First-timers often fail to realize that such teeth are *really* tiny—a quarter to a half inch long. Keep your eyes open. Your search can be made more efficient by use of a trowel and sieve; bring your own or borrow those thoughtfully provided by the park. Low tide makes access to the intertidal gravels easier.

Swimming is allowed at this small beach, but space fills up quickly on hot summer days. Behind the beach, under the shade of the forest trees, are several picnic tables and a portable toilet. Be sure to bring your own drinking water. Although you can return to your car by the same Red Trail, hikers will enjoy a somewhat longer route on the Orange Trail, which traverses a less-visited section of the park.

To access the Orange Trail, walk inland from the beach for about 100 yards and turn right. Follow the graveled road to the top of the hill and look for the marked starting point of the Orange Trail (the graveled road proceeds due west from here, returning to the parking lot in a direct fashion, and may be used by mountain bikers). The Orange Trail has a few short, steep hills as it winds its way through the forest in a circuitous fashion. Mountain laurel and American holly are still plentiful, forming the understory of a mature forest with many tall tulip poplars. Much of Calvert Cliffs State Park is a designated Wildlands, defined by the Maryland General Assembly as "containing wilderness characteristics and otherwise outstanding and unique natural features worthy of preservation in a natural state." An especially noteworthy feature of this trail is its lack of non-native, invasive plant species that so plague the huge majority of hiking trails in Maryland.

After almost two miles, the Orange Trail emerges from the forest within sight of Route 765. Bear left along the edge of an agricultural field, and then follow a park service road for 0.4 miles back to the developed section of the park.

Directions

From the Baltimore Beltway (I-695), take Route 3/301 south to Route 4, near Upper Marlboro. From Washington, DC, take the Route 4 exit off the Capital Beltway (I-495). From the Route 4 / Route 3 intersection at Upper Marlboro, continue south on Route 4 for about 30 miles. The entrance to Calvert Cliffs State Park is well marked and comes just after the entrance to Calvert Cliffs Nuclear Power Station.

Other Outdoor Recreational Opportunities Nearby

Flag Ponds Nature Park is located just a few miles to the north and has hiking trails and a mile of beachfront for swimming.

MIOCENE FOSSILS

Although fossils may be found in several areas of Maryland, by far the best-known deposits are those at Calvert Cliffs and the adjacent Chesapeake Bay shoreline. Indeed, these eroded bluffs yielded the first American fossil (of the mollusc *Ecphora gardnerae*) to be described in the scientific literature, all the way back in 1685. Since then, generations of scientists, knowledgeable amateur collectors, and curious citizens have searched the cliffs and the wave-tossed gravels at their base for fossilized shells, shark teeth, and whatever else the action of wind and water might erode out.

(continued)

The animals whose remains form these fossils lived long ago. Between 10 and 20 million years ago, during a geological epoch called the middle Miocene, a shallow ocean covered much of what is now southern Maryland. Its waters lapped gently against a shoreline located just east of present-day Washington, DC. The climate was warmer than it is now, more similar to that of modern South Carolina, and forests of scrub oak, pine, and bald cypress dominated the dunes and marshes along the shore. Out in the fairly warm, calm waters of the ocean, a profusion of plants and animals lived and died, linked in a complex food chain. The shells, bones, and teeth of dead animals, resistant to bacterial and chemical degradation, settled gently to the bottom, where they were covered with mud and fine sand. Over time, mineralization may have occurred, fossilizing the remains, but some shells and teeth remained unaltered. Sediments containing these fossils built up for millions of years into a 300-foot-thick band now known as the Chesapeake Group. More than 600 species of fossilized plants and animals have been classified from these sediments, including molluscs, arthropods, fish, reptiles, birds, and mammals.

Many of the fossil-containing cliffs in Calvert County are private land, and access to them requires permission. Even so, digging is never allowed, as this would hasten the rate of erosion. For these reasons, the fossils most commonly found are shark's teeth gleaned from the shoreline gravels at public beaches adjacent to the cliffs. They range in size from tiny teeth a few millimeters long to five-inch monsters from an extinct species of great white shark. Small teeth are plentiful and, once you develop an eye for them, easy to find. Indeed, it's hard to believe that this many sharks could have lived here. To explain this abundance, recent studies have shown that sharks replace their teeth as often as every eight days. Whatever the origin of this paleontological bounty, it represents a window into Maryland's past that never fails to excite the imaginations of young and old alike.

American Chestnut
Land Trust: Parkers Creek

County: Calvert

Distance: 4.2 miles as described; circuit hike

Difficulty: Easy to moderate. Hilly; sandy terrain

Dogs: Permitted on leash

Why It's Special: A lovely coastal plain deciduous forest surrounding a pristine estuarine creek

More Information: American Chestnut Land Trust, www.acltweb.org, (410) 414-3400

Street Address: 676 Double Oak Road, Prince Frederick, Maryland 20678

GPS Coordinates: 38.546795, 76.532340 (trailhead)

The American chestnut tree is all but gone from the Maryland landscape. Once a co-dominant member of our forest tree community, as large and omnipresent as oak and hickory, beech and tulip poplar, the chestnut was valued both for the quality of its wood and the usefulness of its autumn fruits. Chestnut blight, a fungal disease accidentally introduced into the eastern United States more than a century ago, killed an estimated 4 billion chestnut trees. By 1940, the only chestnuts still surviving were isolated individuals separated from any other chestnut (and its blight) by more than six miles, and even fewer trees with some degree of partial immunity to the disease. A few chestnut trees in the latter category still stand in the western part of central Calvert County, their specific location known only to a handful of conservationists. The American Chestnut Land Trust was founded in 1986 to preserve these trees and the forested acreage surrounding them. Since then, the Trust has expanded its role, managing adjacent tracts owned by the Nature

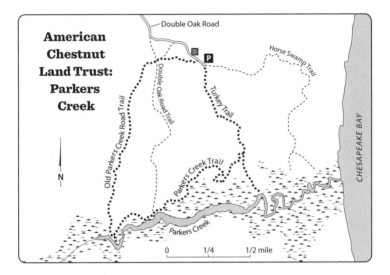

Conservancy and the State of Maryland, and providing public access to those lands.

And a fine job the Trust has done. They own or manage more than half of the 7,321-acre Parkers Creek watershed, renowned as both the most pristine watershed on the western shore and as a microcosm of Chesapeake Bay. In its 2.5-mile length, Parkers Creek encompasses bayfront cliffs, sand beaches, marshes that grade from brackish to fresh, wooded swamps, and riparian and upland forest. Most significantly for hikers interested in visiting this remnant of pre-colonial Maryland, the Trust maintains more than fifteen miles of trails open 365 days a year.

The Parkers Creek Loop Trail may be the most enjoyable of the various hikes on ACLT property. It encompasses pleasant upland Coastal Plain forest, glimpses of the steep ravines so characteristic of Calvert County, and views of the Parkers Creek marsh from the adjacent riparian forest. This circuit totals almost five miles, the longest trail at the ACLT.

Trip Description

Begin your hike from the Double Oak Farm trailhead, site of the ACLT office, on what is known as the "North Side" of the preserve. (There is also a network of shorter trails on the "South Side" of

Parkers Creek, accessed by a different road from the highway, Route 4, through Prince Frederick.) Portable toilets are located here, and there is a pleasant porch on the nearby barn for rest and relaxation. Be sure to sign in at the trail register; visitation figures are valuable to the ACLT when applying for grants and other funding vehicles. The Parkers Creek Loop is blazed in purple and begins just across the dirt road from the barn.

This first segment is called the Turkey Trail. It runs along a narrow ridge in a southerly direction through a forest of tall trees dominated by tulip poplar, American beech, and hickory. Large vines climb far up these trees and may eventually pull down those host trees that are small or weakened. The understory is thick with spicebush and some American holly, but no mountain laurel. The contrast with the trails of Calvert Cliffs State Park, just a dozen miles to the south and with a similar soil type, topography, and aspect, is quite striking; mountain laurels virtually line all the trails at Calvert Cliffs. Spring wildflowers are not particularly plentiful here at the ACLT, since the more upland areas that now constitute the preserve were farmed until the 1930s.

After 0.6 miles, a trail intersection is reached. Continue downhill on what is now called the Turkey Spur for a third of a mile to its end at the Parkers Creek marsh. Here the sinuous nature of Parkers Creek is evident as it forms curves that wind through the marsh. At this point, where the marsh is at its widest, you will find a good place to watch for resident birds of prey: osprey and bald eagle, both common in the Parkers Creek watershed. After enjoying the view, return to the above-mentioned trail intersection.

Turn left (west) on what is now called the Parkers Creek Trail but is still blazed in purple. The first few hundred yards follow the hilltops, but eventually the trail dips down to marsh level and runs along that ecotone. A screen of trees often obscures views into the marsh, but a few pocket wetlands keep the terrain interesting. Pass the Double Oak Road Trail (which merely returns straight uphill to the trailhead), reaching the Bridge Spur after 2.7 miles.

This is the site of an old bridge across Parkers Creek, extant until the 1930s. Only the vertical support pilings are still visible; it's amazing that they are still here after almost a century submerged in mud and water. From this point, walk uphill on what is called the Old Parkers Creek Road Trail (still blazed in purple and a part of the Parkers Creek Loop). Decades of wagon and horse traffic have incised the old road into man-made ravines that dissect the land. These shady defiles often support Christmas ferns, mosses, and lichens. The forest along the Old Parkers Creek Road Trail is a younger one, with less impressive trees and some invasive plants. After 1.4 miles of uphill travel, the gravel entrance road is reached. From this point, it is only 100 yards by road back to the trailhead, but the ACLT has recently put in a short trail through the woods that is about twice as long and affords views of several steep ravines that are so typical of this landscape.

The ACLT lands on both sides of Parkers Creek are a part of the largest block of unbroken forest in Calvert County. As such, they form a valuable laboratory against which the effects of fragmented development can be measured. For example, some animals require large tracts of unbroken forest to live and reproduce. Called FIDS (forest interior dwelling species), birds like Kentucky warblers and wood thrushes are doing well here but declining elsewhere. While it may not be evident to the casual observer, places like Parkers Creek are truly special.

Directions

From Washington, DC, take exit 11A off the Capital Beltway (I-495/I-95), Maryland Route 4. Proceed for 31 miles to Prince Frederick,

Maryland. Turn left on Dares Beach Road. Go 2.5 miles. Turn right on Double Oak Road and drive to the end. From Baltimore, take Route 3/301 south from the Baltimore Beltway (I-695) for 30 miles. Exit onto Route 4, heading east toward Prince Frederick, going 23 miles. In Prince Frederick, turn left on Dares Beach Road. Go 2.5 miles. Turn right on Double Oak Road and drive to the end.

Other Outdoor Recreational Opportunities Nearby

The American Chestnut Land Trust also has trails on the south side of Prince Frederick and Parkers Creek. There are signs on Route 4 directing you to these locations.

CHESTNUT TREES AND CHESTNUT BLIGHT

The forests that cloaked most of Maryland at the time of John Smith's explorations were very different from the forests that exist today. Not only were there extensive tracts of huge old trees, shading the forest floor in a dim, filtered sunlight, but the kinds of trees in those forests were different. In particular, the stately American chestnut tree was an ecological dominant, representing about one out of every four trees on many upland sites. Colonists found it perhaps their most useful tree, for it grew fast and tall, split easily with a straight grain, was rot resistant, and was easily worked. Its wood was used for fence rails, siding, rough-cut boards, and furniture, and its meaty nut fed both people and animals. The chestnut is gone now from Maryland forests, eradicated by disease within living memory of our older citizens. Will we ever be able to restore the American chestnut to its former glory, the tree taking its rightful place in the canopy of our old forests?

The trouble began in 1904, when a scientist at the Bronx Zoo noticed several of the zoo's chestnut trees dying. The trees displayed cankers on the bark, abnormal growths with an orangish

(continued)

cast. The origin proved to be an infection caused by the chestnut blight fungus, *Cryphonectria parasitica*. The fungus enters the living part of a chestnut tree through a wound or minor damage and begins to flourish. It sends out long threadlike filaments, known as hyphae, that grow, fuse, and eventually choke off nutrient distribution, killing the tree. Unfortunately, the chestnut blight spread steadily as fungal spores were carried on the wind and on the feet of birds. By the 1930s almost every chestnut in the Appalachians was infected and soon died.

Since then, the chestnut has been mourned by those who remember its grandeur, and it has not been forgotten. Hope for its reestablishment comes from several sources. First, there are a small number of native trees that are genetically resistant to chestnut blight; the fungus infects these trees but is unable to kill them. Such trees will become important breeding stock, contributing their genetic heritage to a completely resistant strain in the future. Second, a virus that infects the chestnut blight fungus was discovered in Europe in the early 1950s. This virus causes the fungus to be less virulent, and such "hypovirulent" strains typically allow the tree to survive. Unfortunately, the virus cannot "cure" every strain and variety of chestnut blight, and so it is currently of only limited usefulness. Finally, the techniques of molecular biology are now being applied to curing chestnut blight. The physical damage to the tree is caused by the secretion of oxalic acid by the fungus. Scientists have cloned into chestnut cells a gene from wheat that codes for an enzyme (oxalate oxidase) that breaks down oxalic acid into harmless products. While this result is promising, much work still needs to be done before scientists can say they have a "cure" for chestnut blight. Still, scientists are hopeful that such advances will spell new hope in the restoration of one of our forest giants.

Patuxent River Park:
Jug Bay Natural Area

County: Prince Georges
Distance: up to 9 miles, depending on route; circuit hikes
Difficulty: Easy. Mostly flat but with a few slight hills; sandy terrain
Dogs: Permitted on leash, except in the Black Walnut Nature Study Area
Why It's Special: A diverse landscape of upland forest, swamps, and marshes, filled with birds and wetland vegetation
More Information: Prince Georges County Department of Recreation and Parks, http://outdoors.pgparks.com/Sites/Jug_Bay_Natural_Area.htm, (301) 627-6074
Street Address: 16000 Croom Airport Road, Upper Marlboro, Maryland 20772
GPS Coordinates: 38.773210, 76.710644 (Visitor Center)

The Patuxent River drains a large chunk of central Maryland real estate, and it is the only major watershed entirely within the borders of the Free State. In that sense, the Patuxent can be called Maryland's river. From the rolling fields and ever-increasing suburbia of Howard County, to the protected forests of Patuxent National Wildlife Refuge and Fort Meade, to the extensive wetlands and farmlands surrounding the lower river, the Patuxent embodies much of what has been called "The Land of Pleasant Living." That slogan may have originated in a beer advertisement, but even so, there is much truth in it.

The best and most accessible place on the Patuxent is in the vicinity of Jug Bay. Here the river spreads out into a broad estuary in the rough shape of an old-fashioned whiskey jug when viewed from the air. Owned and operated by the Maryland-National Capital Park and Planning Commission, Department of Parks and Recreation of Prince Georges County, the Jug Bay Natural Area is over 2,000 acres and has about eight miles of natural surface trails. The freshwater marshes of Jug Bay are some of the highest quality and most diverse wetlands in the state. Taken together, the land and water host a great variety of plant and animal life. A visit to Jug Bay Natural Area is very worthwhile as a hiking destination (with options for cycling and paddling as well).

Trip Description

At the Jug Bay Visitor Center there are restrooms, drinking water, information, displays, and brochures, as well as friendly and knowledgeable staff. Just outside the Visitor Center is a handicap-accessible tower, newly constructed in 2016, that provides views over the wide marshes of Jug Bay. A few steps away are the short trails of the Black Walnut Nature Study Area; this is a fine place to begin your hike, especially if you enjoy birding and botanizing. These short walking paths and boardwalks connect to the large trail network on surrounding park lands.

Begin your hike at the trailhead behind the restroom building. The upland forest here features large, mature trees like American beech, sycamore, tulip poplar and several kinds of oaks, with an understory of spicebush and American holly. The steep ravines here precluded logging, preserving these trees and their woodland habitat for decades. Turn right at the first trail intersection, which is in the valley of Black Walnut Creek. Upland forest gives way to a swamp forest, with water-tolerant trees like red maple, bald cypress, and black gum, and herbaceous plants like jewelweed, skunk cabbage, and royal, hay-scented, and interrupted ferns. Much of the trail becomes boardwalk, keeping your feet dry and preventing damage to the delicate swamp vegetation.

The trail crosses the tiny creek on a footbridge, continues down the other side of the stream, and soon reaches a beautiful but small freshwater marsh. (A swamp is a wetland with trees, while a marsh has only shrubs and herbaceous vegetation.) There is a beaver lodge here, and wood ducks and great blue herons are frequent visitors. Shrubs like arrowwood, button bush, alder, and winterberry create a complex three-dimensional structure to this marsh, while blooming

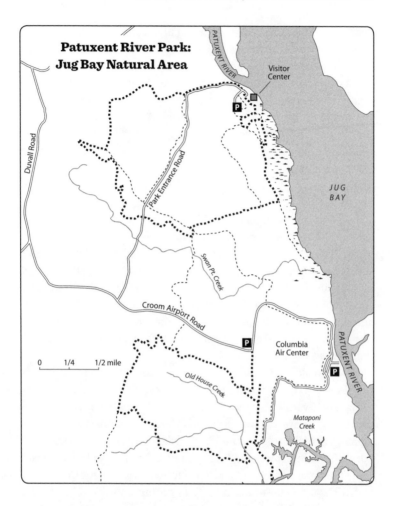

**Patuxent River Park:
Jug Bay Natural Area**

PATUXENT RIVER

Visitor
Center

P

Duvall Road

Park Entrance Road

JUG
BAY

Swan Pt. Creek

Croom Airport Road

0   1/4   1/2 mile

P

Columbia
Air Center

PATUXENT RIVER

Old House Creek

P

Mataponi
Creek

crimson-eyed rose mallow, pickerelweed, spatterdock, cardinal
flower, and tickseed sunflower all lend color to the scene in season.
Even though this trail is (so far) less than 200 yards long, there is a
lot to see and observe, so take your time, walk quietly, and stop often.

The trail now leaves the valley of Black Walnut Creek and runs
downstream along the Patuxent, the sandy trail occupying the ecotone between forest and marsh. There is a wooden deck with pretty
views of the main river and its marshes, and then the trail turns
uphill onto the Coastal Plain plateau. While global warming may
increase sea levels, the land in the Jug Bay Natural Area is mostly

twenty to thirty feet above the current high water line, and so should remain secure for centuries to come.

Join the Green Trail, marked by fiberglass posts with color coded arrows, and turn left. Walk through a maturing forest on a wide fire road for a quarter mile. At this point, turn right, still on the Green Trail; if you continue straight, that arm of the Green Trail merely ends at a scenic overlook now grown up in trees so that there is no longer anything to see. The Green Trail runs dead flat and wide for another half mile before reaching more interesting terrain.

From this point, you have several hiking options. I recommend two.

For a four-mile loop that ends at the Visitor Center, leave the Green Trail and turn left on the Red Trail. Within 100 feet, turn right on the Blue Trail. The Blue Trail is the narrowest of all the trails at Jug Bay, a true backcountry trail just wide enough for a single person. It is only lightly used by horses. The Blue Trail follows the terrain up and down short hills, hitting every point of the compass. After 1.3 miles, it ends near the park border. Make a hard right and join the Purple Trail, which is an old dirt fire road. At a trail junction, bear left (both directions are the Purple Trail).

The Purple Trail now runs along a meadow, the edge of which has filled with fast-growing sweet gum trees. Sweet gums are easily recognized by their five-lobed, star-shaped leaves that turn purple in autumn. They are a southern tree of Coastal Plain sandy soils, rarely found west of the I-95 corridor in Maryland. After almost a mile, the Purple Trail intersects the Park Entrance Road. Turn left and walk along the broad road shoulder for 0.4 miles to the Visitor Center.

Still want to do more hiking? I recommend you drive to the southern half of the Jug Bay Natural Area to do a pleasant 3.4-mile loop around the edges of the Old House Creek watershed. Turn left on Croom Airport Road from the Park Entrance Road, and follow it about two miles to a gravel parking lot at a T intersection. Park under a massive bur oak, an uncommon species in Maryland that is easily recognized by the fringe on its large acorns.

Walk down the paved road toward the group camping area. The large field to your left was once an airfield, first called Riverside Field, then Columbia Air Center. Opened in 1941, it was the first airfield on the East Coast owned and operated by an African American, John Greene. The airport closed in 1956. At the barn and picnic shelter,

turn left, walking across the grass for about 100 yards to a gap in the treeline. This marks the Orange Trail; walk a quarter mile to its junction with the Red Trail.

At this point, a small diversion is in order. Take the adjacent paved road downhill for 100 yards to a wooden bridge over Mataponi Creek. Almost 400 yards long, this sturdy bridge gives you a birdseye view of a shrub-filled swamp, a marsh, and finally the creek itself. Autumn, when the red fruits of winterberry and swamp rose ripen and the leaves of arrowwood and black gum turn crimson, is an especially beautiful time.

Return uphill on the paved road and rejoin the Red Trail, bearing left, away from the road. Turn right on the Blue Trail, which at one point drops steeply to a footbridge crossing an arm of Old House Creek. This steep-sided, narrow vale seems a secret and private retreat, given the fairly flat terrain of the surrounding coastal plain. The Blue Trail eventually emerges from the woods, skirts a cornfield, and reaches a dirt road that is the Green Trail. Turn right, following this trail for almost a mile. Turn right on the Orange Trail, which completes the rectangular course of this hike at the barn and picnic shelter. This circuit is just over three miles in length.

For those with a great deal of energy, these two circuits can be combined into one hike of nine miles in length. If you consider each circuit to be the plate of a dumbbell, a part of the Green Trail would be the shaft connecting the two plates.

Directions

From Baltimore, take the Beltway (I-695) to Route 97 south for 11 miles. Take exit 7 to Route 3. Continue on Route 3 for 9 miles; it becomes Route 301 at this point. Continue another 12 miles on Route 301. Turn left on Croom Station Road.

From Washington, DC, take the Capital Beltway (I-495) to exit 11A, Route 4. Go 8 miles. Turn onto Route 301; go 1.7 miles to Croom Station Road and turn left.

Once on Croom Station Road, go 1.6 miles. Turn left onto Croom Road. Go 1.5 miles. Turn left onto Croom Airport Road. Go 2 miles to the Park entrance. The Visitor Center is 1.7 miles down the Park Entrance Road.

Other Outdoor Recreational Opportunities Nearby

Canoes and kayaks may be rented seasonally from the Visitor Center and launched from nearby Jackson's Landing; paddling the nooks and crannies of Jug Bay is especially rewarding for those who love nature. While the area described in the hikes here is on the west side of Jug Bay and the Patuxent River, it is also worth visiting the east side, home to Jug Bay Wetlands Sanctuary, where there are hiking trails and excellent opportunities for wildlife viewing. Neither should be confused with Patuxent River State Park, which lies several dozen miles upriver in Howard and Montgomery Counties.

HORSESHOE CRABS

They come on the rising tide, strange armored creatures crawling out of the small waves and up the beach, black against the sand. There are a few at first, then more, and soon the water's edge roils and churns with their bodies. Foot-long spikes spear the air; the whipped foam is a mix of seawater and semen as the breeding frenzy continues. Just beyond the highest high tide line, females scoop out shallow depressions in the sand and lay several thousand greenish-black eggs, each perhaps a millimeter in diameter. Horseshoe crabs by the thousands have arrived on the shores of Delaware Bay on this afternoon in late May, and they are the last great wildlife spectacle in the mid-Atlantic region.

Although the epicenter of horseshoe crab breeding is on the beaches of Delaware and New Jersey, Marylanders too are familiar with these strange-looking arthropods. Lesser numbers of horseshoe crabs use several remote Maryland beaches for egg laying, including those behind the Atlantic barrier islands and the islands of the lower Chesapeake Bay. Their shells litter these beaches year-round, the subject of great interest by beachcombers of all ages.

Horseshoe crabs are sometimes called living fossils. Cambrian rocks from 450 million years ago contain horseshoe crab fossils, their form virtually unchanged from those we see today. That such a creature can remain so similar for so many eons speaks to their evolutionary success and adaptability.

For most of the year, horseshoe crabs are anonymous to us humans, prowling the ocean shallows offshore, dining on shellfish and marine worms buried in the sandy or muddy sediments. Only when they breed in late May do they enter our consciousness, but they do so in a remarkable way. A day spent on a horseshoe crab breeding beach is a never-to-be-forgotten experience.

The female horseshoe crabs lumber ashore on the high tide and lay their eggs just above the high tide line so that their eggs do not get swept away by repeated tidal washings. Nevertheless, many of these eggs never get the opportunity to hatch because they are eaten by gulls and shorebirds. In particular,

(continued)

semipalmated sandpipers, dunlins, ruddy turnstones, and red knots, birds that migrate from South America to the Arctic each spring, rely on this bounty of horseshoe crab eggs to complete their journey.

Two other aspects of horseshoe crab biology are noteworthy. First, their blood (called hemolymph) is used by the health care industry in a test for bacterial contamination of drugs and medical devices. When exposed to even the tiniest number of bacteria, the hemolymph clots to create a visible gel. Anyone who has ever received a vaccination has had the vaccine tested for bacterial contaminants using the horseshoe crab agglutination test.

Second, horseshoe crabs have a unique visual system, with a total of ten "eyes" of six different types. There are two compound eyes of the sort found in many insects, located atop the shell. Also located atop and around the edge of the shell are two other kinds of eyes, each sensitive to different wavelengths of ultraviolet light. There are photoreceptors on the telson (spiky tail) that merely sense certain wavelengths of light but are not true eyes. Median and ventral eyes complete the visual suite. Horseshoe crabs are extremely sensitive to low light levels; the structures that contain the visual pigments, rods and cones, are one hundred times larger in size than those of humans. The world perceived by a horseshoe crab is remarkably different from what you and I see.

If you have never been to a horseshoe crab beach in late May, be sure to go soon. In the first few years of the twenty-first century, overharvesting of horseshoe crabs (used by watermen as bait) reduced their numbers significantly. At that same time, shorebird species dependent on the eggs also saw their numbers reduced; the red knot, in particular, became a candidate for the federal Endangered Species list. A ban on horseshoe crab harvests by New Jersey and Delaware has permitted the numbers of both kinds of animals to bounce back, but the future is always uncertain. Resolve to visit this year to experience the last great wildlife spectacle in our area.

Rock Creek Park

County: Washington, DC

Distance: 10.2 miles as described; circuit hike

Difficulty: Moderate. Generally rolling with a sandy treadway, but hilly and rocky in places

Dogs: Permitted on leash

Why It's Special: A surprisingly pleasant but heavily used urban park that actually seems quite wild and remote on some parts of the trail

More Information: Rock Creek Park, www.nps.gov/rocr, (202) 896-6070 (Wednesday–Sunday only, 9 a.m.–5 p.m.)

Street Address: None available for trailhead

GPS Coordinates: 38.986791, 77.052454 (Boundary Bridge trailhead)

Rock Creek Park in Washington, DC, is a true treasure for those who live in that congested city. It is an urban oasis and an island of natural habitat amid a sea of concrete and cars. At 1,754 acres, almost three square miles, Rock Creek is one of the largest urban parks in America. Although the park is heavily used, it is still possible for visitors to experience a real sense of solitude, even isolation, while hiking a backcountry trail. Rock Creek has been preserved as a national park for more than 125 years. For this reason, much of the park is heavily wooded, populated by really big, mature trees. In ecological terms, it is approaching an old-growth forest: that is, one that contains a multi-layered, multispecies canopy, upright dead trees (snags), diverse and complex sub-canopy, sapling and seedling layers, much woody debris on the forest floor, and complex soils rich in organic materials with active nutrient cycling. And while it helps to be able to recognize the unusual features of this forest, anyone can appreciate the tall trees and heavy shade that buffer trails from the encroachments of civilization. A hike in Rock Creek Park is a surprisingly pleasurable outing.

The Valley Trail and the Western Ridge Trail together form a 10.2-mile circuit traversing the best natural areas of Rock Creek Park. Several minor connecting trails and roads with wide grassy shoulders permit shorter hikes for those with less time or energy. On weekends, large segments of Beach Drive, the paved road running due north/south through the heart of the park, are closed to motor vehicles. This paved route is very popular with cyclists, in-line skaters, parents with children in strollers, and casual walkers. Indeed, on weekends and federal holidays it is possible to travel from the District of Columbia's northernmost point to the Potomac River near the Mall on pavement, without sharing the road with motor vehicles.

Trip Description

This hike begins at Boundary Bridge, just off Beach Drive, at the northern border of Rock Creek Park. This location is a convenient access point for anyone using the Capital Beltway (I-495) to reach the park. Citizens living in the District of Columbia probably have their own favorite ways to enter Rock Creek Park. There is a small parking lot at Boundary Bridge, and there are several other lots just north of this point along Beach Drive.

Walk just a few yards downhill from the parking area and cross Rock Creek on the Boundary Bridge. The Valley Trail is on Rock Creek's floodplain, and the rich alluvial soils host perhaps the finest display of spring wildflowers within the District's borders. There are extensive gardens of Virginia bluebells here, delicate sprays of sky-blue, funnel-shaped flowers hanging from arched stems. Other springtime ephemeral woodland wildflowers common here include spring beauty, trout lily, bloodroot, Dutchman's breeches, wild ginger, and several kinds of violets. Unfortunately, lesser celandine, an extremely invasive non-native ground cover, has flourished here over the last few decades, gradually replacing the native wildflowers. Hikers have created a network of trails, further contributing to the demise of wildflowers by trampling and soil compaction. Still, this is a beautiful place, even if overused.

Follow the trail along Rock Creek, looking for light blue blazes on trailside trees. Vernal pools on the floodplain support the eggs of

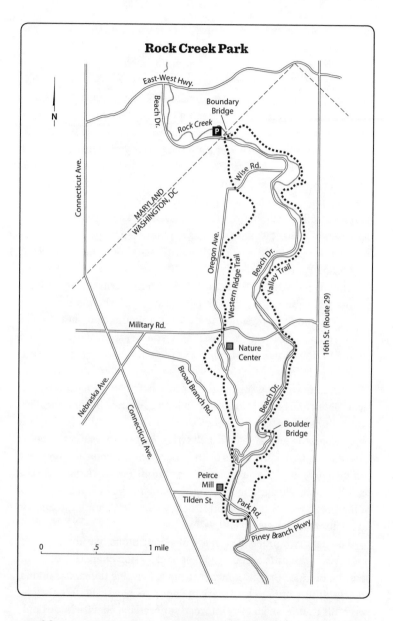

Rock Creek Park

wood frogs, spring peepers, and American toads. The chorus of these amphibians can be quite loud on a warm rainy night in March. By early May, a variety of migrating songbirds like warblers and vireos sing from the trees overhead. With wide, flat trails and good habitat, this is a favorite location for birding. After about a mile or so, the Valley Trail narrows a bit and alternates between running along the floodplain and on the adjacent hillside. Several hundred yards below the second footbridge across Rock Creek, look for a small sign that says "foot traffic only." This is the official Valley Trail, but contrary to information on the park map, this trail actually disappears for a few dozen yards, requiring a walk in the roadway of Beach Drive. So instead, continue on the wider trail that brings you to Beach Drive at the Milkhouse Ford bridge. Cross the road with care and take some time to enjoy the grassy lawn shaded by large trees. In summer, this is a busy place, with families picnicking, kids and dogs playing, and couples strolling. When Rock Creek Park was established by order of Congress in 1890, it was set aside as a "pleasure ground for the benefit and enjoyment of the people," and this spot is a prime example of its intended use.

The Miller cabin is found at this location, perhaps the only remaining log cabin within the District of Columbia's boundaries. Built in 1883 by the then-popular but now mostly forgotten poet and essayist Joaquin Miller, it was used as a getaway from the bustle and stench of downtown Washington in summer. Poetry readings are sometimes held here.

Continue walking south on the grass between Beach Drive and Rock Creek and cross Military Road with care. Just beyond the Park Police Substation, the blue blazes of the Valley Trail appear again on trees on the east side of Beach Drive. This also marks the point where Rock Creek drops its calm, meandering façade and begins a tumultuous journey over the hard crystalline boulders that give the park its name. The gradient increases, and for the next mile a series of ferocious rapids develop after heavy summer thunderstorms or late winter snowmelt.

The next two miles of trail are of a continuously rolling nature, but none of the hills exceed 100 feet of elevation change. Along this section, Boulder Bridge comes into view. Perhaps the most famous, and certainly a unique, landmark in Rock Creek Park, Boulder Bridge was built in 1902 of steel-reinforced concrete faced with large boulders of local stone. Legend has it that while the contract called for stones capable of being *lifted* by a man, the contractor misread the document and installed boulders *as big as* a man. The effect was salutary, however, and so was not corrected. The bridge cost $17,634.77, a princely sum then, but it has withstood the test of time and is beloved by generations of Washingtonians.

After 5.6 miles, the Valley Trail ends with a crossing of Beach Drive and the Bluff Bridge footbridge across Rock Creek. Now on the west side of the creek, the return trail that runs generally northward is called the Western Ridge Trail and is marked by sea-foam green blazes. Almost immediately, the trail splits, offering the hiker a "moderate" trail or a "strenuous" trail. The moderate trail is hilly but with a smooth treadway, while the strenuous trail has two places where hands must be used to scramble up several feet of rock face and a few dozen feet where there is an acrophobic dropoff trailside to the waters of Rock Creek. It's not really all that difficult, but take your choice. The two arms of the trail reunite a quarter mile farther at Peirce Mill.

Peirce Mill is a beautiful large building of native stone once used to mill wheat into flour. It was the centerpiece of a thriving family business in the first half of the nineteenth century and just one of at least eight such mills along Rock Creek in that era. A sluiceway diverted water from the river and used it to power a waterwheel. It is surprising how little water was needed to turn the large wheel, which generated 20–40 horsepower of torque.

Just beyond Peirce Mill, the trail rises from the floodplain to the ridge, perhaps 200 feet higher in elevation. At Equitation Field (a fenced ring for training riding horses), bear left; this is one of the few places on the Western Ridge Trail where blazes are missing. This area of the park contains stabled horses and related facilities. President Ronald Reagan reputedly rode here to briefly relieve the pressures of his office.

Just beyond the Horse Center, where the trail crosses Military Road, are the remains of Fort DeRussey. One of a series of earth and log forts that were constructed during the Civil War to protect the Union's capital, Fort DeRussey looked out from the high ground over what were then open fields and farmland. The cannons of the fort were effective in repulsing an attack by Confederate forces on July 11–12, 1864.

From this point on, the remaining three miles of the Western Ridge Trail is a wide, well-graded, immaculately maintained path. For most of that distance, the trail passes through a mature forest with large trees, many with a diameter greater than two feet. Oaks dominate on dry slopes, while tulip poplars are the most common tree where the soil is richer and a bit more moist. There are occasional gaps in the canopy where a forest giant has crashed to earth under the influence of time, wind, and gravity, permitting light to reach the forest floor and allowing fast-growing saplings to colonize that space. However, like many forests in urban and suburban areas, by 2010 there were relatively few tree seedlings on the forest floor in Rock Creek Park. White-tailed deer numbers had increased from zero in the late 1950s to more than 100 per square mile at the start of this century, a density almost tenfold higher than is ideal. These deer ate virtually every seedling and the leaves of any plant within their reach.

These changes in vegetational cover also affected animals that use the forest. For example, hooded warblers and Kentucky warblers, two bird species that nest in shrubs less than six feet off the ground, disappeared from Rock Creek Park within a few years after white-tailed deer returned. Wood thrushes, once so common here that this beloved species was designated the official "state" bird of Washington, DC, have also declined dramatically.

Starting in 2012, the park instituted a program to cull the deer population to a level where the forest can recover: where seedlings can grow large enough to survive to maturity, where wildflowers can again set seed and reproduce, and where there is sufficient habitat for ground- and shrub-nesting bird species. Only time will tell if the program will be successful.

The Western Ridge Trail continues in a northward direction, bordering the well-kept houses of Oregon Avenue for a block or so and then dropping into the shallow valley of Pinehurst Branch. After another mile of upland trail, the pathway descends into the Rock Creek Valley at Boundary Bridge, concluding this 10.2-mile hike.

President John Quincy Adams walked the trails of what became Rock Creek Park in the early 1800s, and so did President Theodore Roosevelt a century later. Today, another century along, hikers not only walk in the footsteps of these renowned men but can experience some of the same qualities they so appreciated: the play of sunlight on just-greening leaves, the mists of an early summer morning rising from the creek, the song of thrush, vireo, and warbler enriching the spring season. There is still much to cherish in this urban gem called Rock Creek Park.

Directions

From the Washington, DC, Capital Beltway (I-495/I-95), take exit 33, Connecticut Avenue. Turn right (north) at the stoplight. Go about 100 yards; turn right on Beach Drive. Follow Beach Drive for 2.5 miles to the trailhead at Boundary Bridge.

Other Outdoor Recreational Opportunities Nearby

On weekends, Beach Drive is closed to motor vehicles and is a popular venue for cyclists, runners, etc. From Peirce Mill, near the southernmost point on this hike, you may continue south on the paved Rock Creek Trail to the National Zoo, the start of the C&O Canal towpath, and the National Mall.

SILENT SPRING REVISITED: THE DECLINE OF FOREST SONGBIRDS I

More than fifty years ago, Rachel Carson's landmark book *Silent Spring* ushered in a new age of environmental awareness, exposing the dangers of DDT to wildlife and human health. Its influential message was a clarion call to action, and the public clamor it created resulted in a ban on DDT and its poisonous relatives. Since then, many of the most severely affected bird species, like bald eagles and peregrine falcons, have made dramatic recoveries.

More recently, however, a new threat to birdlife has appeared, and scientists now realize the magnitude of the problem and its implications. Many of the species of songbirds that form our most beautiful avifauna have been rapidly declining in numbers. In particular, species that nest in the deciduous forests of North America and winter in Mexico, Central and South America, and the Caribbean are affected the most severely. Called neotropical migrants, most of the warblers—as well as many thrushes, orioles, and tanagers—are in trouble throughout their range. Overall, the total number of individuals of these species is declining at the rate of about 1 percent per year.

(continued)

The plight of forest songbirds here in Maryland is no better and is perhaps worse than that in other states throughout the eastern half of the nation. Anecdotal evidence for reduced numbers of neotropical migrants abounds; just ask any longtime birder. More rigorous proof, evidence from scientific studies analyzed statistically, is harder to come by. Nevertheless, some good records exist in cases in which sites with mature, undisturbed vegetation have been monitored by dedicated groups of volunteers for more than forty years. The best records are from sites in downtown Washington, DC: Rock Creek Park and Cabin John Island in the C&O Canal National Historical Park.

Both of these sites, less than ten miles apart, are on federally owned land preserved forever from development. Cabin John Island is a mature floodplain forest of 18 acres; the Rock Creek site is much larger, consisting of 66 acres of upland deciduous forest. Experienced birders visited these sites between mid-May and mid-June, the peak nesting season, and sought to identify every breeding pair of birds on the tracts.

The data are unequivocal. For the Cabin John Island site, the density of breeding pairs (expressed per 250 acres) averaged about 260 in the 1940s, 1950s, and 1960s, with little variation between decades. By the early 1980s, the average was 130, exactly half. In Rock Creek Park, the statistics are even more grim: about 85 pairs per 250 acres in the 1940s, 1950s, and 1960s declined to 35 in the early 1980s. Most important, the decline was almost exclusively among neotropical migrants; year-round local residents and short-distance migrants like robins and blue jays held their own. In the early years of the census, neotropical migrants formed 60 to 80 percent of the breeding pairs; recently, they composed less than 40 percent. On a disheartening note, Hooded warblers, Kentucky warblers, black-and-white warblers, and yellow-throated vireos are extinct at these places. Several other species are present in some years but not others, or are present at extremely low densities relative to the past. Clearly, these forest-dwelling species are in trouble; their conservation is a test of our resolve to coexist peaceably with the full spectrum of organisms that share Maryland, our nation, and our planet.

North Point State Park: Black Marsh

County: Baltimore

Distance: 5 miles as described; circuit hike

Difficulty: Easy. Flat; generally well-drained terrain, with a few muddy spots

Dogs: Permitted on leash, on trails only

Why It's Special: Beautiful Chesapeake Bay views, a pristine freshwater marsh, and a unique history of human activity make this park well worth a visit

More Information: North Point State Park, http://dnr.maryland.gov /publiclands/Pages/central/northpoint.aspx, (410) 477-0757

Street Address: 8400 North Point Road, Edgemere, Maryland 21219

GPS Coordinates: 39.220605, 76.430339 (trailhead)

North Point State Park is an anomaly. Although it is perhaps the last large chunk of undeveloped, pristine upper Chesapeake Bay waterfront, it sits almost in the shadow of the former Bethlehem Steel, once Maryland's largest smokestack industry. Owned by the state since 1987, this 1,310-acre tract was significantly upgraded in 2000, with improved trail signage and development of an asphalt bike path. In addition to being ecologically significant, North Point has had a rich human history in ancient, colonial, and recent times. And this unique natural area is located within just a few miles of the Baltimore Beltway.

The area owes its informal name to the 232-acre Black Marsh, which with its surrounding 435-acre forested buffer forms a designated State Wildland and Natural Heritage Area. The marsh proper is considered to be among the best examples in the state of a tidal freshwater marsh. It harbors a wide diversity of birds, including bald eagles and rare American bitterns. In temperate weather, the marsh is a refuge for wading birds such as herons and egrets, whose habitat around Bay waterfront is becoming increasingly stressed by encroaching civilization. In winter, waterfowl such as canvasback, goldeneye, ruddy ducks, mergansers, and scaup congregate here. Black Marsh is home to eight species of flowering plants that are considered endangered or rare and in need of conservation.

North Point State Park's human history dates back at least 8,000 years. Although generations of locals have discovered arrowheads and pottery shards along eroded shorelines and in cultivated fields, a more formal but still preliminary archaeological survey yielded campsites, workshops, shell middens, and a village from the Late Woodland period.

Recorded history began when Maryland was settled in the 1600s. Todd's Inheritance, a plantation of several thousand acres on the North Point peninsula, included Black Marsh and was the first recorded residence in Baltimore County. The house was at least partially burned by the British in 1812 and today it is listed on the National Register of Historic Places. The area was in the British line of advance (and later retreat) in the campaign that culminated in the Battle of North Point.

More recently, a portion of the property south of the marsh proper was developed as the Bay Shore Amusement Park. Long a landmark for Baltimoreans, Bay Shore opened in 1906 and served several generations for forty-one years. Today, all that remains are the old trolley barn, the central fountain, the 1,000-foot Bay Shore Pier, and much slag, rock, and cobble fill along the shore.

The development of this relatively new Maryland State Park was the subject of great controversy in the 1990s. The State of Maryland wanted to develop the park intensively along the Chesapeake Bay, building a marina, boat slips, and an amphitheater. Conservationists argued that any development should be placed away from the water, in consonance with the state's own Critical Areas regulations. They further argued for traditional park uses rather than those that attracted large numbers of people. In part because of budgetary considerations, the state abandoned its intensive development plan. In 2000, the old haul road was paved, the bike path was built, and the trolley barn and fountain were restored. The result is a quiet and beautiful park featuring natural values.

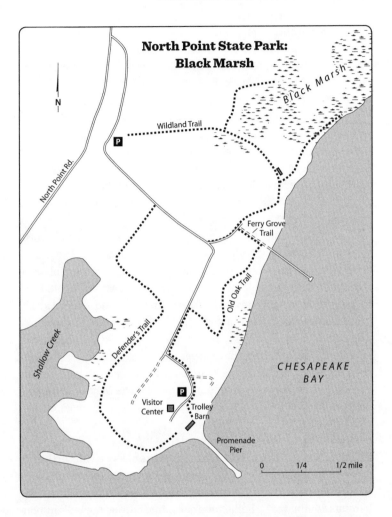

The walk described here totals about five miles over flat but occasionally muddy terrain. In warm weather, bring along insect repellent.

Trip Description

Start your hike from the parking lot adjacent to the entrance station a short distance from North Point Road. The Wildland Trail begins from one corner of the parking lot and is blazed in white. Initially the trail passes through what was once an agricultural landscape, now grown over in shrubs and small trees. A row of mulberry trees lines the path, its wine-dark berries staining the ground in June. The trail soon emerges into the open space of Black Marsh. Access is by the old trolley roadbed that once brought visitors to Bay Shore Park. Constructed of slag and other waste fill from Bethlehem Steel, the trail allows hikers to see a freshwater marsh up close without getting wet and muddy. The marsh has a unique beauty in all seasons, but midsummer is probably the best, when thousands of crimson-eyed rose mallows blossom extravagantly across the wetland. These huge flowers, members of the hibiscus family, have large white petals whose interior throat is lined with a bright red pigment.

The trail reenters forest and soon reaches a side trail well worth a detour. This footpath, blazed in light blue, leads to an observation deck yielding wide views across the marsh. This is a good place to search for birds, especially in migration, both spring and fall. Look for great blue herons, snowy and American egrets, red-winged blackbirds, and an assortment of gulls. Black Marsh was once home to a population of black rails, sparrow-sized birds that are so rare and elusive that most birders have never seen one. Unfortunately, black rails no longer nest at Black Marsh, part of a decades-long decline in numbers of this most uncommon species. The Maryland Department of Natural Resources added black rails to its endangered species list in 2007.

Return to the Wildland Trail and turn left, proceeding through a forest dominated by short but ancient white oaks of wide girth. The forest here is a mix of low, wet places that support moisture-loving plants, such as royal fern, jewelweed, and red maple, and higher, drier habitats dominated by hollies and oaks. Just beyond the hulking concrete shell of the old powerhouse, once used to generate electricity that ran the trolley, turn left on a lightly used trail.

This detour is quite worthwhile, ending at a long arc of isolated Chesapeake Bay beach. It is a fine place to look for gulls, ducks, and shorebirds. The long views across the Chesapeake remind us of how unusual and valuable a stretch of undeveloped beach really is. After exploring the shoreline, return to the Wildland Trail.

Continue walking south as the trail curves away from the water, eventually bearing left onto the blue-blazed Ferry Grove Trail. At its end, the old concrete ferry landing attracts loafing gulls and cormorants in all seasons. Proceed south on a foottrail that winds through a forest rich in large oaks and hollies, eventually reaching the park road. Turn left to reach the developed portion of North Point State Park.

Located on the Chesapeake, this area was the site of Bay Shore Park. Very little is left of what was once a busy place, fondly remembered by older Marylanders. There is a modern Visitor Center that contains old photographs and artifacts from the glory days of Bay Shore Park. The trolley barn has been refurbished as a picnic pavilion, and nearby the formal fountain has been charmingly and lovingly restored.

Near the trolley barn but at the water's edge, walk out onto the jetty that was once the promenade pier. Jutting out more than 1,000 feet into the Bay, the pier affords excellent views of the northern Chesapeake. A few hardy, stunted trees cling to a precarious existence on the thin soil, exposed to the prevailing winds and storm tides of Chesapeake Bay.

Returning to the mainland, you'll find a stone-surfaced bike trail at one end of the trolley barn. Known as the Defender's Trail, it winds through forest and field, eventually passing your parking lot near the entrance station. Should you wish to hike farther on this trail, it continues for 2.2 miles west to North Point Boulevard.

Directions

From the Baltimore Beltway (I-695) take exit 43. Make a left at the first blinking light (Bethlehem Boulevard). Continue for 1 mile, crossing over North Point Boulevard onto North Point Road. Go 1.9 miles to the park entrance.

Other Outdoor Recreational Opportunities Nearby

The Defender's Trail at North Point State Park is mostly paved and suitable for cycling, although there are three road crossings where care must be exercised. Bikes are not allowed on the Wildland Trail.

BLACK RAILS

Black rails may not be the rarest species of bird in Maryland, but they are probably the least frequently seen. Only the most dedicated birders include a black rail on their life lists. Even scientists who study this elusive species are frustrated by the secretive nature of black rails, and there is much about the life history of black rails that is unknown.

A black rail is about the size of a house sparrow and is black to dark gray in plumage with white speckles on the back. Only the legs and large, strong toes exhibit any color, a yellowish green; they dangle awkwardly during flight. Like all rails, black rails have a narrow body that can be further compressed as needed, hence the expression "thin as a rail."

Black rails live in salty, brackish, or freshwater marshes. For this reason, the several species of rails are sometimes called "marsh hens" or "mud hens." The largest population of black rails in Maryland is probably on the lower Eastern Shore, in the extensive cordgrass marshes of southern Dorchester County around Elliott Island. Black rail populations are best censused by sound at the start of the breeding season, when males call just after sunset and before dawn. Their "kik" or "did-ee-dunk" note is distinctive, but so obscure was this bird that its call was not associated with the species until 1958. Fortunately for scientists and birders, males will respond to a tape-recorded call. In fact, black rails have been known to attack the speakers on a tape recorder. Black rails are so difficult to see that standard procedure is to avoid movement after playing the recording for fear of stepping on a bird. The typical sighting is a brief glimpse of a small, mouse-like bird darting through the vegetation and disappearing in a blink. Compounding the difficulties of observing black rails is the fact that the best time to see them is at night in the lonely, bug-infested marshes of early summer.

Black rails nest in a cup of soft grasses that often arches overhead. These nests are next to impossible to find; one researcher, who spent an entire summer in the field, never discovered a nest. The first published photographs of a female black rail on a nest appeared in 1987, and the photographer noted that this was the first time in thirty years that a nest had been found. Six to eight eggs are usually laid, but little is known about the incubation time and the time to fledging. Insects, seeds, and marine crustaceans are common food items. By late October, black rails have migrated to their wintering grounds along the southern coast of the United States, although a few may stay in Maryland throughout the winter. Even though reputedly weak fliers, black rails somehow complete this migration twice a year, in an anonymous fashion.

Our lack of knowledge about black rails precludes active management for their conservation. Right now, preservation of known black rail habitat, on both the breeding and the wintering grounds, is about all that can be done. The effects of marsh disturbances like ditching, burning, invasion by non-native species, and insecticidal spraying on black rail populations are completely unknown but worrisome. Sea level rise in the Chesapeake region has already reduced the high marsh habitat favored by this species. Black rails remind us that wildlife management is still an inexact science and warn us that hubris regarding our understanding of the natural world is largely unwarranted.

Lower Susquehanna Heritage Greenway Trail

County: Harford

Distance: 7.2 miles as described; out-and-back hike

Difficulty: Easy. Flat; part gravel multi-use trail, part sandy backcountry trail

Dogs: Permitted on leash

Why It's Special: The alluvial floodplain surrounding Chesapeake Bay's largest feeder river has superb displays of spring wildflowers and many migrating songbirds, while the area near Conowingo Dam is the best place on the East Coast to view bald eagles in late autumn

More Information: Susquehanna State Park, http://dnr.maryland.gov /publiclands/pages/central/susquehanna.aspx, (410) 557-7994

Street Address: Near 4390 Rock Run Road, Havre de Grace, Maryland 21078 (Rock Run trailhead)

GPS Coordinates: 39.608046, 76.142406 (Rock Run trailhead)

B irding and botanizing are two of the favorite activities of hikers who get out into natural Maryland. The Lower Susquehanna Heritage Greenway Trail along the west bank of the Susquehanna River in the northeastern corner of the state is among the best for both of these two pastimes. In April, the alluvial floodplain along the river, and its adjacent slopes, harbor a dense assemblage of beautiful wildflower species. By late April into early May, migrating songbirds, notably warblers, find this habitat an especially favorable location to rest and refuel. Also in spring, anadromous fish like shad and river herring return up the Susquehanna, and the mouth of Deer Creek is a popular place for anglers seeking to fill cooler and creel with these seasonal delicacies. And in November and December, the area below Conowingo Dam is arguably the best place in the mid-Atlantic region

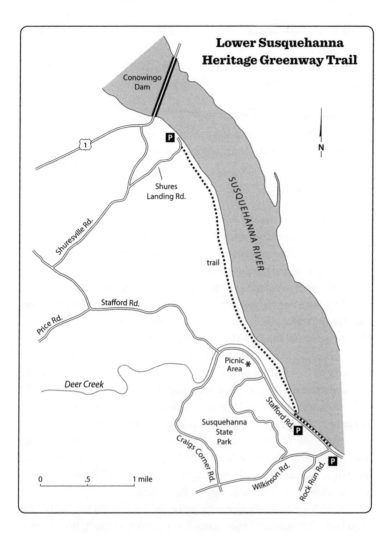

Lower Susquehanna Heritage Greenway Trail

to view bald eagles. Perhaps no other location in Maryland is a more celebrated destination for birders and wildflower lovers.

The hike described here traverses both public and private land and represents an unusual cooperation between private industry and state government. The winners, fortunately, are all of us. Exelon Power in particular is to be congratulated for its preservation of the unique habitats, including alluvial flats and steep, rocky slopes, that extend downriver from Conowingo Dam. The site is known officially as the Shures Landing Wildflower Viewing Area. Exelon

Power provides basic amenities at the dam as well as protection of the resource.

This hike is an easy one over flat terrain. About half of this trail is a wide, all-weather, packed gravel path suitable for bicycles and even strollers. The southern portion of the trail, however, is merely a footpath that is sometimes muddy in places. The distance from Rock Run in Susquehanna State Park, at the southern trailhead, to Conowingo Dam, at the northern end, is just over 3.5 miles.

Trip Description

The hike begins at the Rock Run Historic Area in Susquehanna State Park. There is limited parking here; in the event that all the spaces are taken, continue driving northward on Stafford Road, where there are a number of parking areas over the next half mile. Rock Run has been an area of commercial activity since late in the eighteenth century. The impressive Rock Run Grist Mill was built in 1798 and partially restored in the 1960s. The remains of the Susquehanna and Tidewater Canal may also be seen here and along most of the trail. It was built in 1836 and functioned for almost sixty years. During the construction of Conowingo Dam in the 1920s, a temporary railroad was laid atop the canal's towpath, and the remains of the rails are still visible in the Rock Run area. Rock Run was also the site of a toll bridge across the Susquehanna River between 1817 and 1857. A frame structure here known as the Jersey Toll House is sometimes open for tours. Finally, a beautiful fourteen-room stone mansion built in 1804 graces the hillside overlooking the mill. Both restrooms and drinking water are available at Rock Run.

From the mill, walk north (upstream) on the old towpath/railroad bed. The sporadic ties make for an awkward gait, but there is usually a lot to see in this area, so a slow pace is actually beneficial. Rock Run is the only grassy area along this stretch of river, so there are more birds here than elsewhere. Look for indigo buntings and goldfinches in particular. The trail also supports a number of botanical delights. Expect to see such winsome spring wildflowers as trillium, Dutchman's breeches, Virginia bluebells, spring beauties, and spring cress. Watch where you walk, however, as both poison ivy and stinging nettles impinge on this narrow section of trail.

After a half mile on the old towpath, the trail crosses Deer Creek

Photographing bald eagles at Conowingo Dam

on a sturdy footbridge supported by the railroad piers. Before following this, however, walk across Stafford Road for a look at the adjacent steep hillside. In April, trilliums cover this slope in high density. Trilliums are robust plants with large showy flowers, so called because the major structures are grouped in threes: three leaves, three creamy white recurved petals, and reproductive structures in clusters of three. This is an example of a locally common wildflower. Trilliums, as well as all other species within its genus, are rare or uncommon elsewhere in Maryland east of the mountains. Even within a few hundred yards of these productive colonies, there are none to be found. Apparently some unique combination of physical factors and lack of human disturbance has created the perfect habitat for these floral gems.

Interspersed among the trilliums are Dutchman's breeches, another uncommon wildflower found only in rich, well-developed woodland soils. These white flowers are aptly named; each looks like an inverted set of pantaloons, and several hang from an upright pole. Although Dutchman's breeches are not as rare as trilliums in Maryland, they are still uncommon—and darn cute.

The footbridge over Deer Creek is a fine place to look for birds as well. Its elevation above the water puts you closer to the treetop haunts of warblers, vireos, and other less frequently observed songbirds. Phoebes and swallows nest under the bridge. Out on the Susquehanna, great blue herons often hunt the shallows, while double crested cormorants frequently loaf on midstream rocks. The distinctive chirp of an osprey signals the presence of one of these large fish hawks soaring overhead, and a bald eagle may occasionally drift past. At river level, fishers of another kind are present from dawn until dusk; this is a prime spot for humans to wet a line. During spring migration upstream, anadromous fish like shad and herring seem to pause at the mouth of tributary streams like Deer Creek, perhaps explaining why this spot is so popular with the rod-and-reel set.

Passing over the bridge, walk onto the peninsula of land between Deer Creek and the Susquehanna River. During the month of April, this special place is home to many dozens of acres literally carpeted with Virginia bluebells. Clusters of sky blue, bell-shaped flowers hang downward; the leaves are succulent with smooth edges. Some of the plants exhibit mutations in flower color; albino plants have white flowers and a few are magenta in hue. Bluebells are common in the right habitat in Maryland: river alluvial floodplains like those along the Gunpowder and Potomac. Here, however, they grow in a profusion unequaled elsewhere, and wildflower enthusiasts often make an annual pilgrimage to Susquehanna to see its bluebells.

Virginia bluebells, trilliums, and Dutchman's breeches are known as ephemerals because they are visible to us for only about a month each spring. They grow rapidly in early April, taking advantage of the direct sunlight hitting the forest floor through the leafless trees. They flower, set seed, and die back after canopy closure in May. They spend the other ten months of the year as rhizomes or roots, quiescent beneath the forest floor. Other well-known springtime ephemerals of the forest include trout lilies and spring beauties.

As the early spring flowers fade, this forest becomes popular with another group of naturalists: birders. Early May is peak spring warbler migration, and many of these tiny and elusive birds follow river valleys in their northward journeys. For this reason, these alluvial forests along the Susquehanna are among the best places in Maryland to see these active, beautiful birds. Flying at night and resting during the day, warblers glean small insects from the sun-dappled treetops. Most birders identify warblers, as they flit rapidly from tree to tree, by their distinctive and usually complex calls.

Although spring migrants prompt the heaviest birdwatching activity, any time of year has its rewards. Ospreys return to the Susquehanna each spring. Their distinctive, high-pitched mewing call often attracts attention to them as they soar over the river. Kingfishers are common over the river in all seasons, as they seem to be along almost every watercourse in Maryland. Waterfowl, including wood ducks, geese, and mallards, can also be seen. After a mile, this narrow woodland path joins the Lower Susquehanna Heritage Greenway Trail. About a dozen feet in width with a hard-packed gravel surface, the trail's remaining two miles are popular with cyclists and runners and quite suitable for small children and those with physical challenges.

The left side of the trail is wetland, ranging from shallow water to merely soggy soil, populated by twisted box elder trees. Although it is hard to discern now, this area was once a barge canal, built in 1838 as part of an extensive network of such waterways connecting the tidewater to the fertile farmlands of central Pennsylvania. On the opposite side of the path, the river is nearby, shielded from view only by a thin screen of vegetation. Fishing trails frequently lead down to the water, providing access to a broader sweep of view. Large silver maples and sycamores line the shore itself, hardy survivors of high water events (although true floods have been moderated by the dam). Native spring wildflowers are not as common here as along the more downstream portions of the trail, having been displaced by a variety of non-native, invasive plants like garlic mustard, lesser celandine, and Japanese knotweed. Even so, it is a pleasant and shady walk.

After 2.2 miles of this graveled trail (3.6 miles from Rock Run), a gate marks the northern terminus of the Lower Susquehanna Heritage Greenway Trail. Ahead is a parking lot at the base of Shures Landing Road, with space for more than a hundred cars. This area at the base of Conowingo Dam is extraordinarily popular with fishermen in all seasons and at all hours, taking advantage of the special artificial habitat. In winter, the water passing through the turbines creates an ice-free spot in even the coldest weather. In spring, anadromous fish migrating up the river to their spawning grounds in Pennsylvania and New York are blocked by the dam, providing an artificially high population density. In summer, the oxygen-rich, aerated water attracts fish from the upper Chesapeake Bay, where algal growth sometimes depletes the water of life-giving oxygen. At peak times, fishermen jam the shoreline cheek by jowl. You may also see Exelon biologists at work on their fish lift project. In an effort to restore and increase spawning stocks of anadromous fish, migrants are removed from the river, placed into aerated tanks, and trucked to the upstream side of the dam, where they are released. In a recent enhancement of this project, Exelon Power spent $12 million and has the capacity to transport 750,000 American shad and 5 million river herring. Amenities in this area include picnic tables, trash cans, and wheelchair-accessible portable toilets.

The area at the base of the dam is also incredibly popular for birding in late fall. In late November, it is the best place in the mid-Atlantic to see bald eagles. It is not unusual to have several dozen eagles in view, some in the big sycamores that shade the parking lot where they can be clearly seen even without binoculars. The eagles are relatively easy to photograph here, and on sunny mornings at this time of year there are often several hundred serious photographers with huge tripod-mounted lenses awaiting just the right moment.

After enjoying both the avian and human sights at the dam, return to your car at Rock Run by the same route for a total hiking distance of 7.2 miles. On the return trip, during spring migration, birders will want to visit the Susquehanna State Park picnic area, a renowned hotspot for warblers. Instead of getting off the graveled trail at the sandy path that leads back to Rock Run, continue a half mile on the Lower Susquehanna Heritage Greenway Trail to its southern terminus at Stafford Road. Cross the bridge over Deer Creek and walk 100 yards south along the road to the entrance to the picnic area. In early May, experienced birders may observe more than a dozen species of warblers in this area alone. Return to the trail by the same route. This detour adds an extra two miles of walking to your hike.

Directions

From Baltimore or Washington, take I-95 north. Take exit 89; turn left (west) on Route 155. Go about 2 miles and then turn right on Route 161. Go a short distance and then turn right on Rock Run Road. The trailhead is located at the gristmill at the terminus of Rock Run Road.

Other Outdoor Recreational Opportunities Nearby

There are several good hiking trails covering the hills above the river in Susquehanna State Park.

CONOWINGO DAM AND AMERICAN SHAD

One of the earliest signs of spring is the return of anadromous fish like shad, alewives, and herring to streams and creeks of the Chesapeake Bay watershed. Tales of these migratory fish in colonial times, when the Bay was only lightly impacted by human activities, seem unbelievable to us today. A common statement was that the fish were so thick "a person could walk across a stream on their backs and never get wet feet." The migrating fish arrived just in time for spring planting, and it is said that farmers would dig a hole, drop in a seed, and toss in a fish as fertilizer. After a long winter of preserved foods, Marylanders embraced fresh fish as an especially welcome addition to the early April diet. The favorite among these fish was the American shad, a toothsome if bony finfish that was often pinned to a wooden plank and roasted near an open fire.

American shad spend most of their lives in the Atlantic Ocean, where they feed on plankton and other tiny sea creatures. However, they spawn and lay eggs in freshwater streams, migrating up to several hundred miles to reach the creek where they were born. In the Chesapeake watershed, American shad once spawned as far north as Cooperstown, New York, near the headwaters of the Susquehanna River. And unlike salmon, American shad do not die after breeding but return to the sea, repeating the cycle in future years. These immense journeys capture our imaginations and engender a sense of wonder, and for these reasons American shad hold a special place in piscatorial lore.

But all is not well with the American shad and some other anadromous fish. Although water quality in Chesapeake Bay may play a role, the primary culprit is the series of four dams on the Susquehanna River that block access to spawning grounds on shallow, upriver tributaries. For example, in 2015, only 43 American shad made it past all four dams, and only 13 river herring made it past Conowingo Dam. The decline of fisheries and fish stocks is an old story, but this one is far more complicated than it might at first appear.

(continued)

In the early 1990s, two programs were instituted to help fish get past these dams. First, fish "elevators" were installed, essentially cages lowered into the water at the base of the dam and then hauled to the top for release into the reservoir behind each dam. The one at Conowingo cost the dam's owner, Exelon, over $12 million. Second, Exelon operated a fish taxi service, pumping water and fish from the base of Conowingo Dam, trucking them several dozen miles, then releasing them above the fourth dam. By 2001, success seemed imminent; nearly 200,000 American shad and almost 300,000 alewife and herring passed through the lift. The taxi service was discontinued.

In the next decade, however, something unexpected happened. Numbers of American shad taking the fish lift declined at a steady pace, reaching the paltry numbers described above in just fifteen years. Worst of all, scientists have only guesses regarding why the fish lift has ceased being effective. It's not that very few American shad are arriving at the base of Conowingo Dam. Biologists count fish in the Susquehanna River each spring, and more than 100,000 American shad crowded the river below the dam. There are lots of fish in the "lobby"; it just seems that something is keeping them from boarding the "elevator." And with so few American shad reaching their spawning grounds, the population is bound to crash at some point in the near future.

Pink Lady's Slipper orchids. There are more than 28,000 species of orchids, and more than 50 reside in Maryland. None are more numerous (although still uncommon) and showy than pink lady's slippers, typically found under pines in mature forests. The Adkins Arboretum has a significant population that is regularly monitored.

Painted trillium. This handsome member of the genus *Trillium* can be found in Maryland only in Garrett County in rich, undisturbed forests. The Lostland Run Trail is especially blessed by this and two other species of trillium.

Black bear and cubs. Black bears were once virtually extirpated from Maryland, but are now fairly common in the westernmost counties. Seeing one in the wild is still a thrill. Garrett County near Swallow Falls State Park and Cranesville Swamp are prime habitat for Maryland bruins.

Deep Run Trail (*facing page*). Not often hiked, this trail in the Green Ridge State Forest allows access to a designated wilderness thick with herbs, shrubs, and tall trees.

Canopy closure. As trees leaf out in late April, they draw large quantities of water from the soil. Their shade changes the habitat of the forest floor, and springtime ephemeral native wildflowers finish blooming.

Hay-scented ferns (*facing page*). A common fern of lightly shaded forests with rich soil, the delicate foliage of hay-scented ferns belies their hardy nature.

Fameflower. Maryland's most unusual habitat is the serpentine barrens of Soldiers Delight. Flowering for only a few hours in the heat of early July on barren rock, fameflower is pollinated by small bees.

Willet (*facing page*). Willets are a common sight at Assateague Island, their noisy "pee wee willet" call and flashing white and black underwing plumage making them conspicuous. Although willets nest in salt marshes, they are often seen foraging on the beach.

Common raven. Namesake of Baltimore's football team, there is nothing common about the common raven. Large, intelligent, social birds, ravens prosper in wilderness and near towns in the western counties of Maryland. Green Ridge State Forest is prime habitat for ravens.

Lostland Run Trail (*facing page*). Following the stream of the same name that tumbles off the Appalachian Plateau toward the Potomac River, the Lostland Run Trail features beautiful river valley views, a dramatic cascade, and lush gardens of wildflowers rarely found elsewhere in Maryland.

Cranesville Swamp. A boreal bog in extreme western Maryland, Cranesville harbors flora and fauna found nowhere else in the state. A boardwalk permits dryshod passage through the swamp.

Timber rattlesnake. These shy reptiles are not often seen by hikers, but any encounter is an adrenalin-spiking event. Rattlesnakes in Maryland will usually attempt to get away rather than strike—usually. Keep an eye peeled for these and other snakes on the Appalachian Trail and the Kendall Trail.

Tuckahoe State Park. The only true hiking venue on Maryland's mid–Eastern Shore, Tuckahoe features well-maintained trails traversing a mature forest surrounding a Coastal Plain creek. A portion of the route passes through Adkins Arboretum, where signage identifies trees and other plants.

Box turtle. Our most familiar turtle, kept as a summer pet by generations of Maryland children, is common but declining in numbers as their forest habitat is lost. The red iris identifies this individual as a male. Box turtles may be found across Maryland.

Spiderwort. Because they have been domesticated for gardens, it is perhaps surprising to see spiderworts growing along remote trails in habitats where they get sufficient sunlight and soil moisture. Three blue petals and yellow pollen make identification easy. The trail to Maryland Heights has a thriving population of spiderworts.

Lichen (*facing page*). Lichens are common throughout Maryland on rocks and tree trunks. They are a symbiotic pairing of a fungus and an alga or cyanobacterium. This particular lichen, *Lobaria pulmonaria*, is known from only a few locations in Maryland. Lichens are common at Sugarloaf Mountain and the Monroe Run Trail, to name but a few places.

Fawn and doe, white-tailed deer. Maryland's most familiar large mammal, white-tailed deer are common everywhere, having learned to happily coexist with humans. Their browsing has caused extensive changes in the composition of the forest wildflower and shrub community, especially in suburban parks where hunting is not permitted.

Great Falls Tavern Walk and the Billy Goat Trail

County: Montgomery

Distance: Great Falls: Less than a half mile; out-and-back hike

Billy Goat Trail (section A): About 3 miles as described; circuit hike

Difficulty: Great Falls: Easy. Flat; part sandy gravel, part boardwalk

Billy Goat Trail: Difficult. Extremely rocky, strenuous hike

Dogs: Great Falls: Permitted on leash

Billy Goat Trail: Dogs not recommended

Why It's Special: Impressive Potomac River gorge with waterfalls and rare bedrock terrace forest; scenic C&O Canal and towpath

More Information: C&O Canal National Historical Park, www.nps.gov/choh, (301) 767-3714 (Great Falls Tavern Visitor Center)

Street Address: 11710 MacArthur Boulevard, Potomac, Maryland 20854

GPS Coordinates: 38.999286, 77.246098 (Great Falls Tavern Visitor Center)

The most dramatic landscape in Maryland is not some remote mountaintop view far to the west; instead it is found almost within sight of the Capital Beltway. Great Falls of the Potomac is a world-class scenic attraction within a thirty-minute drive of more than a million people. Here the great river drops more than 60 feet over a series of waterfalls and steep rapids, carving a vertical-walled gorge through living rock. The wild landscape dwarfs the many visitors who scramble over rock fins and down steep chutes in pursuit of the ultimate view.

More than just scenery highlights the Great Falls area. It is a part of the C&O Canal National Historical Park, and mankind's mark on the land has been important. Several canal locks are clustered here, one of which is operational. The canal's towpath, parallel to the river, is popular among joggers, cyclists, and walkers. For the naturalist, a large number of habitats cluster within a small area, making birding and botanizing superb. The Great Falls area has the highest density of rare plants and animals in Maryland. Taken together, the many points of interest and the extraordinary ecology and natural beauty make Great Falls a must to visit.

Two hikes are described here. One is better for families with small children, for those with physical challenges, or for those who want to see a great deal of scenery without walking far. The second is a true adventure hike that is probably the most challenging and beautiful in this book.

Trip Description

Great Falls Tavern Walk

Begin this easy stroll from the Great Falls parking lot of the C&O Canal National Historical Park. There are hundreds of parking places here, but on prime spring weekends they may fill by 11 a.m., even though an entrance fee is charged. On such days, arrive early or late in the day; the rest of the year rarely sees such heavy usage, and space is almost always available. A snack bar open on summer weekends borders the parking lot and is the first building you will encounter. A bit farther east is the restored Great Falls Tavern, a massive whitewashed structure dating from 1828, which houses a few basic displays; information is available from rangers inside. Wheelchair-accessible but aging and odorous bathrooms are in a separate building out back. Water is available in the Tavern.

Great Falls Tavern faces a still-functioning lock that is active in warm weather. The Park Service offers authentic mule-drawn canal barge rides; the rides start here and pass through the lock and continue upstream. This is a popular activity so reservations are recommended to avoid disappointment. If you miss out on the canal barge rides, another option is an interpretive hike led by a park ranger. Departing frequently from the tavern area, such walks are invariably informative and worthwhile.

To explore the area on your own, cross the canal on the footbridge just outside the front door of the tavern and turn left. The narrow and busy towpath is wedged between the canal and the Fish Ladder, a narrow chute of the Potomac River where the rocks were long

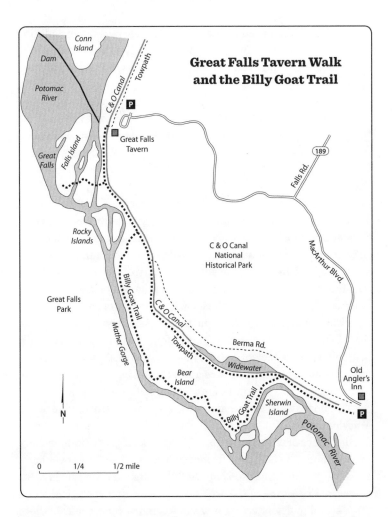

Great Falls Tavern Walk and the Billy Goat Trail

ago modified by engineers in an effort to aid the upstream migration of anadromous fish. Both sides of the towpath have substantial dropoffs, so keep young children firmly in hand in this area. A sign notes that several deaths occur near here each year because of carelessness and poor judgment. The river in particular is very swift, accelerating rapidly toward its plunge over Great Falls.

Continue for about 100 yards and then bear right toward the footbridge to Olmstead Island. Opened in 1992, this wheelchair-accessible bridge replaced a similar one destroyed by Hurricane Agnes in 1972. It first crosses the Fish Ladder. The incredible power of the river is displayed as it explodes in haystacks, recirculating holes, and rock sieves. But this represents only a tiny portion of the Potomac's flow, and even more dramatic views of Great Falls are ahead.

The bridge becomes a boardwalk trail that traverses Olmstead Island and the adjacent Falls Island for almost a quarter mile, passing through a unique natural habitat: a bedrock terrace forest. Dominated by the erosion-resistant rocks that form Great Falls, trees and other vegetation grow only in the cracks and depressions where floods have deposited silt and other alluvium. The same floodwaters that bring a new supply of soil and nutrients may also uproot and wash away trees and herbaceous plants. In fact, a flood of this magnitude occurs fairly frequently; there have been about twenty high-water incidents since 1936 that swept over at least parts of Olmstead Island, and three floods that covered the island entirely. Thus trees never get really big on Olmstead and Falls Islands. Virginia pine, red oak, and post oak dominate the drier sites on the island, whereas pin oak, river birch, and swamp white oak can be found in depressions with poor drainage that makes the soil rather wet. This unique combination of habitats, coupled with the lack of human disturbance, makes these islands home to some of the most rare and unusual herbaceous plants in Maryland. For this reason, be sure to stay on the boardwalk.

The boardwalk terminates at a viewing platform where the Maryland chute of Great Falls is laid out in panorama. This spectacular series of waterfalls is undoubtedly the most striking scenery in Maryland. The falls have formed where the river flows over hard, erosion-resistant rocks and onto slightly softer, more erodable rocks downstream. Aiding in the erosion of these softer rocks is the fact that several faults, or zones of weakness in the rock, occur in these strata. One such fracture zone is the dogleg linking the foot of Great Falls with the Mather Gorge about a quarter mile downstream, visible from this overlook.

Take your time and enjoy the view of the falls. There is good autumn color along the far Virginia shore, and on occasion bald eagles may be spotted soaring overhead; a pair often nests each spring on Conn Island just upstream of Great Falls. Kayakers are often seen surfing, ferrying, and playing in the Observation Deck Rapids just downstream from the foot of Great Falls. Surprisingly, every waterfall and chute of Great Falls has been kayaked, even if only by teams of experts at summer low water. Return to the towpath; hikes both upstream and downstream afford beautiful scenery should you feel like more exercise.

Billy Goat Trail

The Billy Goat Trail, as its name implies, is a challenging hiking trail located just downstream of Great Falls. Families with small children, or those unaccustomed to difficult terrain, should consider carefully whether they want to tackle this arduous trail. But for strong, experienced hikers, the Billy Goat Trail is not to be missed. Kids love the challenge of scrambling over rocks and along cliff edges, even if it makes their parents nervous. I've seen kids as young as five hiking this trail every time I've been on it, and they're invariably having a great time. If everyone in your party is an experienced hiker, the Billy Goat Trail is quite appropriate, and it is as scenic and challenging as any trail in Maryland.

Begin your walk from the Great Falls Tavern, described above. Cross the C&O Canal on the footbridge and then turn left on the towpath, walking in a downstream direction. Pass the footbridge to Olmstead Island and Lock 16. Beyond this point, a fence appears on the right and keeps children and wobbly cyclists from falling more than 100 feet into the Potomac far below. The view from atop this cliff is spectacular. It looks out over a wide section of the Potomac where the river has carved a vertical-walled gorge. Farther along, the river is divided into three channels split by two huge islands, appropriately known as the Rocky Islands. At high water, usually in winter or after major storms, water fills all three channels, but by midsummer low water the two nearest channels are dry.

Within 100 yards of this overlook, the Billy Goat Trail begins, denoted by a sign. In spring there is a diverse collection of wildflowers here, including Virginia bluebells, spring beauty, trout lily, pussytoes, and bluets. The path runs through a landscape studded with boulders and populated with scrubby-looking Virginia pines. Soon the hiker senses open space beyond the pines, and views of the river and its rapids become visible with a short detour off the trail. Eventually, the trail emerges onto flat, exposed rock with spectacular and dramatic views of the Potomac and its gorge. From this vantage point, it is evident that the river has carved its way downward through more than 60 feet of metagraywacke and mica schist, leaving vertical rock walls that are popular with rock climbers. The river fills the entire channel, even at low water, for about half a mile; there is no floodplain. At high water, the river boils in whirlpools, and reflection waves bounce off the canyon walls, creating a chaos of churning, roiling water rushing madly on its way to the sea. This section is called the Mather Gorge; it is named after Stephen Mather, the first director of the US National Park Service.

The trail leads downstream along the top of this barren rock ledge, and it is from this area that the trail gets its name. Hikers must jump from rock to rock, much like a mountain goat. It's a challenging and exhilarating scramble.

Continuing downstream, the Billy Goat Trail winds between forest, scrub, and bare rock. Along the way, there are stream crossings, several beaver ponds, and lots of rock scrambling. At one point, the trail climbs a fracture in the rock so steep that you will need to use your hands for balance. Remember the rock climber's rule: move only one hand or foot at a time, making sure that the other three are firmly anchored.

After almost a mile of travel with views of the river, the trail finally turns inland and away from the Potomac. Fertile alluvial soil has built up here, and in spring an especially rich profusion of wildflowers grows. Hepatica, bloodroot, Dame's rocket, spring beauty, golden ragwort, and especially Virginia bluebells flower brilliantly in April just as the trees are leafing out. While wildflowers are common along the towpath, in few other places are they so abundant and diverse. In fact, Great Falls is generally considered the best place in Maryland to view the greatest variety of spring wildflowers. All too soon this enchanting trail brings you back to the C&O Canal towpath and the end of section A of the Billy Goat Trail.

Turn left onto the towpath to return to your car at Great Falls.

Where the Billy Goat Trail joins the C&O Canal towpath, the canal spreads out into the broad, rock-bound expanse known as Widewater. At one time far back in geological history, this was the Potomac's riverbed, and the builders of the canal utilized this unusual feature. Because the shoreline is so rocky, and its borders are studded with pine trees, the view is reminiscent of a Minnesota northwoods lake rather than a canal just outside the nation's capital. Vultures, ducks, and geese nest on the few tiny islands and on the remote opposite shoreline.

The remaining mile or so on the towpath lacks the challenge and excitement of the Billy Goat Trail, but it is still a very pretty walk. Large trees, dominated by oaks, line the towpath and make it a shady, cool place even on a hot day. Because these forests have not been disturbed for many decades, they harbor a wide variety of birds despite the narrowness of the river corridor within the miasma of suburbanization. Woodpeckers abound, and your chances of seeing the usually uncommon pileated woodpecker are excellent. These crow-sized birds with red crests and white underwings are more often heard than seen, their call louder than that of almost any other bird in the forest. Springtime brings a host of migrating warblers that rest during the day in the insect-rich woods, gleaning their prey from leaves and branches. Although warblers tend to stay near the tops of trees and flit around rapidly, experienced birders can usually locate a number of species. Warbler songs are species-specific and are the best way to identify these tiny visitors.

As you approach the Great Falls area, you'll pass several canal locks, necessary due to the significant change in elevation of the river. The stonework remains, still in relatively good shape after more than 150 years, although the locks are no longer operational. Pass the point where you began the Billy Goat Trail, then the path to Olmstead Island, finishing at the Great Falls Tavern and its adjacent parking lot.

Directions

From Washington, take the Capital Beltway (I-495) west. The final exit in Maryland before crossing the Potomac on the Cabin John Bridge is exit 41, marked Carderock/Great Falls. Proceed 1.75 miles on the Clara Barton Parkway to its end. Turn left onto MacArthur Boulevard. Continue on MacArthur Boulevard for 3.5 miles to its terminus at the sign for Great Falls Park.

Other Outdoor Recreational Opportunities Nearby

From Great Falls Tavern, you can hike 170 miles upstream on the C&O Canal towpath to its western terminus at Cumberland, Maryland, and then continue hiking another 150 miles of off-road multiuse trail (the Great Allegheny Passage) to Pittsburgh, Pennsylvania. The less ambitious may enjoy walking east on the towpath for as much as 14.4 miles to its eastern terminus in Washington, DC. There are also some good hiking trails through the hills surrounding the Tavern; ask at the Visitor Center for details and a trail map.

Bicycling on the C&O Canal towpath in the Great Falls area is possible but not easy. The entire area is often crowded with tourists, dog walkers, and hikers, many of whom seem oblivious to other trail users. Use caution if you bike here. The towpath between the Old Anglers Inn and Great Falls has a 200-yard section that has eroded away and is passable only if you carry your bike over rocky terrain. To avoid this rough ground, the National Park Service encourages bicyclists to use the old Berma Road, found on the mainland side of the canal between the Old Anglers Inn and Lock 16. However, this road is not much better, being very rutted and rocky. Bicycling in the Great Falls area may be more trouble than it's worth. However, riding west on the C&O Canal towpath is both scenic and shady, a most pleasant ride of any distance you choose.

Canoeing or kayaking on the Potomac River between the top of Great Falls and the foot of Little Falls, eleven miles downriver, should be avoided by anyone who wishes to remain alive and healthy. In addition to the obvious dangers of the falls, other more subtle but equally hazardous situations abound, even in areas that may appear benign. Stay off this section of the river. That said, the C&O Canal from the Great Falls parking lot seven miles upriver to Violettes Lock makes an enjoyable trip. It is a pleasant, shady paddle on flatwater through an area rich in wildlife.

MAYFLIES

Evening on the Potomac: the sun has set and the sweet humid dusk of summer settles over the river. Rocks still radiate the heat of the day, but the air is now cool, and the Potomac is calm and mirror-flat in the gloaming. Dimples appear on the river's surface, tiny concentric circles expanding outward. Just above the water, small dun-colored insects mill about; occasionally one drops her abdomen to the water's surface for a moment, creating the dimple, and then flies back upward. Soon more insects appear, and within minutes a living blizzard of mayflies whirls over the river. The early summer swarm is underway, a synchronous frenzy of breeding and egg-laying that will ensure continuation of the species into another year.

The adult mayflies that appear in these breeding swarms make their presence briefly known by their sheer numbers, but for most of their life mayflies are rather anonymous animals. In fact, adult mayflies live for only a few hours to a few days; because of their short adult life, their taxonomic classification has been given the order name Ephemeroptera. There are about 575 species of mayfly in North America, and they are widespread in all sorts of freshwater aquatic habitats where water quality is reasonably good.

Adult mayflies are beautiful creatures. Two pairs of nearly transparent wings are held vertically, and forelegs and tail filaments extend a great distance from the body. Adult mayflies have one purpose only: to breed. They do not feed; in fact, their mouthparts are not functional. Mayflies rely on stored body tissue to supply energy for their brief adult life. After mating, female mayflies lay their eggs singly or in clumps on the surface of the water. The eggs quickly sink to the river bottom and attach to a rock. They grow and develop, eventually hatching out into the larval stage known as the nymph.

A nymph has three distinct body segments: head, thorax, and abdomen, with a pair of external gills found on the middle abdominal segment. It has three pairs of legs and three tails and grows by shedding its exoskeleton. Nymphs are either herbivores or detritivores, grazing on algae or dead vegetable material, respectively. Mayfly larvae are fed upon by fish and by predatory aquatic insects like the larval forms of dragonflies, damselflies, dobsonflies, and stoneflies. As such, mayflies form an important part of the aquatic food chain.

Mayfly nymphs typically spend about a year in the larval form. After their final molt, the body begins to rearrange itself into an adult and eventually floats to the surface. There the adult hatches out, dries its wings, and flies off. Mayflies are very

(continued)

vulnerable to predation in this form, and fish feed voraciously during a mayfly hatch.

Perhaps the most unusual aspect of mayfly hatching is its synchrony. When a hatch occurs, almost all members of a population hatch together, within a few minutes to an hour of each other. Scientists believe this synchronous hatching holds predation to a minimum by saturating the environment with hatching mayflies. Although predators take a heavy toll, only so many mayflies can be eaten in such a short period of time; the rest survive to continue the species by breeding.

Soldiers Delight Natural Environmental Area

County: Baltimore

Distance: Serpentine Trail: 2.2 miles; circuit hike

West side trails: 2.9 miles as described; circuit hike

Difficulty: Easy to moderate. Hilly; rocky terrain

Dogs: Permitted on leash

Why It's Special: Arguably the most unique landscape in Maryland, a serpentine barrens with an unusual geology and soil chemistry that hosts many rare plant species

More Information: Soldiers Delight Natural Environmental Area, http://dnr.maryland.gov/publiclands/Pages/central/soldiersdelight.aspx, (410) 922-3044

Street Address: 5100 Deer Park Road, Owings Mills, Maryland 21117

GPS Coordinates: 39.410200, 76.838831 (Visitor Center)

Soldiers Delight is well known among botanists as one of the great natural areas in the mid-Atlantic states. Underlain by an unusual kind of rock, Soldiers Delight harbors a variety of plant species that are rare, uncommon, or endangered, including fringed gentian, fameflower, sandplain gerardia, and serpentine aster. But even if you're not interested in the unique plant life, you will find it to be among the most beautiful and serene places in Maryland to visit. And it's not heavily used; even many Baltimore-area hikers are unaware of Soldiers Delight.

For many people, the charm of Soldiers Delight lies in its open, prairielike habitat that gives long vistas over meadows of dry, tawny grasses. Copses of pines line swales in the terrain and stud the uplands, lending color and scent to the landscape. From high ground, the westering sun goes down over distant rolling hills, setting a wide horizon afire. There is no other place in Maryland quite like Soldiers Delight.

The land that composes Soldiers Delight totals about 2,000 acres, and most of it is owned by the state of Maryland. It is administered by the Department of Natural Resources as a Natural Environmental Area. Thus, there are no playgrounds, picnic shelters, or other forms of intensive development. There are, however, seven miles of hiking trails and a nature center.

Soldiers Delight is one of Maryland's most unusual place names. Although there are several colorful tales about how the area got its name, the reality is more prosaic. In the 1700s, large parcels of land were often given alluring titles to make them more appealing to buyers.

There are two hiking trails at Soldiers Delight, one on each side of Deer Park Road. While they are easily connected to form a single walk of 5.1 miles, each trail is described separately, since many hikers choose one or the other. These hikes cover rolling, broken terrain but have no large hills. The ground underfoot is frequently rocky, and those rocks have jagged edges. Thus, care should be exercised when walking with small children. Older kids and those who hike with some regularity should have no problem. Horses and mountain bikes are prohibited on the trails at Soldiers Delight due to the sensitive nature of the vegetation. For the same reason, hikers should stay on the established trails.

Trip Description

Serpentine Trail

Begin your walk from the Visitor Center just off Deer Park Road. The parking lot is open from 8:00 a.m. to dusk daily, although the adjacent Visitor Center is open only on Saturdays and "when staff is available." Should you arrive when the Visitor Center is open, take some time to read the displays about the history and ecology of Soldiers Delight. There are wheelchair-accessible bathrooms and water available in the Visitor Center building (entrance is on the back side of the building) any time the gate is open. If the gate is locked, you may park at the large gravel turnout (known as the "Overlook") about 200 yards north along Deer Park Road.

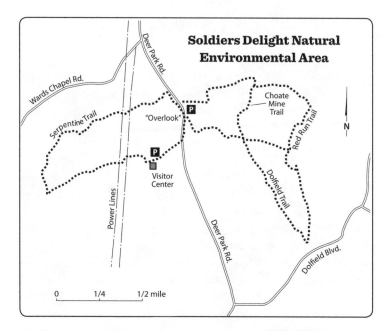

The white-blazed Serpentine Trail begins as a dirt road on the north side of the Visitor Center. This hike is described in a clockwise direction, so turn left, walking away from the parking lot. The trail passes through a dry forest with an understory of mountain laurel that is beautiful in late May but shows extensive browsing by white-tailed deer. In fall and winter, deer are frequently seen in this area as they search for acorns from the large oak trees. Although regulated hunting is allowed at Soldiers Delight, deer have nevertheless reached an unnatural density. White-tailed deer have significant negative effects on shrubs, small trees, and forest ecology. Within 100 yards, the trail comes within sight of Red Dog Lodge, a striking building of natural stone constructed in the first decade of the twentieth century. Once a privately owned hunting lodge, it is now used for storage and the occasional winter program. There are beautiful views over miles of the rolling Piedmont countryside from the Lodge's lawn.

The trail soon emerges into an open area underneath the power lines. Although grasses dominate, there is also a variety of wildflowers, some of which are unique to Soldiers Delight and some of which are common in central Maryland. Because the local utility company

Photo by Esther Fleischmann

must keep trees from growing under the power lines, the area is regularly disturbed. Disturbance gives the seeds of common plants a foothold that they lack in other parts of Soldiers Delight.

Underfoot, notice that the ground is quite rocky. The geology of Soldiers Delight is what makes the area unique and of special interest to naturalists. In few other places is the connection between underlying parent rock, soil, and plant life so direct and easily understandable. The rock at Soldiers Delight is uncommon, containing a mineral called serpentinite. It is rich in magnesium, chromium, nickel, iron, and other heavy metals. Since soils are largely derived from the parent rock, some pockets of soil at Soldiers Delight may contain high concentrations of these toxic metals. In addition, soils here are quite thin. Almost nowhere at Soldiers Delight can you dig down more than an inch or two before striking solid rock. Thin soils hold water poorly and dry out quickly. Together, these austere soil conditions place stress on the plants that grow here, very few species of which can tolerate such harsh conditions. Plants found at Soldiers Delight tend to be those that are well adapted to the unusual soils. Many are unique to Soldiers Delight and similar serpentine-containing soils; at least thirty-eight plant species are categorized as rare, threatened, or endangered in Maryland.

The rocky, eroded footpath continues downhill through a forest of stunted pines. Virginia pines presently cover more than half of the acreage at Soldiers Delight. However, old photographs show that in the 1930s, Virginia pines were largely confined to gullies and swales; the huge majority of acreage was in prairielike grasslands. Since then, pines have gradually shaded out the grasses and wildflowers of the prairie, dominating more and more of the land.

After more than a half mile, the trail bears sharply right and descends into the first of three stream valleys. The path here traverses loose rock of a fragile, easily broken nature that appears tan to white in color. Break off a piece of rock; the interior will be a greenish black. Upon oxidation during weathering, this serpentine-containing rock will turn to its normal, dull appearance. This unusual rock is rare on the East Coast of the United States. Geologists believe that it represents a chunk of the earth's mantle, that semisolid region lying between the crustal plates and the molten core. During certain cataclysmic events like the collision of continental plates, portions of the mantle may have reached the planet's surface at widely spaced locations.

The largest of the three streams, Chimney Branch, is quite shallow but never dries up. It has its origin as a spring just downhill from Deer Park Road. Despite its modest flow, Chimney Branch boasts a surprisingly large and diverse aquatic fauna. The undersides of rocks in gravelly riffle areas will usually yield one or more aquatic insects. Caddis fly, mayfly, beetle, and dragonfly larvae all may be found within a search of a few minutes. Tiny salamanders are common, as are small fish in quiet pools. While some of these animals are grazers on live or dead vegetation, others are predators. Among the most notable, dobsonfly larvae, known to fishermen as hellgrammites, exhibit powerful hind pincers that can sharply pinch a finger. Taken together, these stream animals indicate a complex aquatic food web dependent on continued good water quality buffered by the surrounding undeveloped land.

Streamside soils are deeper, richer, and more moist than those on the uplands. These low, wet meadows are known for their autumn blooming of fringed gentians, flowering sparsely along the water's edge. This delicate herb is unusual not just for its late season, October flowering but also for its American-flag-blue coloration. The fringed petals open only at midday, folding up tightly from midafternoon to midmorning. This most beautiful wildflower has its only occurrence in Maryland along this stream. Unfortunately, these fringed gentians are being loved to death; the ground around them is sometimes trampled and compacted, and the flowers are occasionally picked, in violation of regulations. Please stay on the trail, observe the flowers from afar, and leave them for the next person to enjoy.

After passing through the third swale, the trail rises onto the uplands and bears right. It eventually emerges into a large area lacking trees and dominated by waist-high grasses. For almost a half mile, the trail continues through this sere and harshly exquisite land; evening is especially striking. The rich earth tones of the many kinds of grasses found at Soldiers Delight have a special beauty evident only to those willing to stop and observe closely. Each seed head is actually a complex of many miniscule flowers that require a hand lens to truly appreciate. Botanists identify grasses, as with other, more conspicuous flowering plants, by the structure of these tiny flowers. There may be more species of grasses at Soldiers Delight than on any other site in Maryland. Two species, tufted hairgrass and the vanilla-scented holy grass, have their only occurrence in Maryland here at Soldiers Delight.

In the gaps between grassy areas are true serpentine barrens. At first glance, these appear to be filled with small slabs of rock and are devoid of all life (hence the name *barrens*). But close examination reveals tiny plants hugging the ground. Several of these species are found nowhere else in Maryland. For example, fameflower has pale green, fingerlike, fleshy leaves an inch or two long. The leaves are present for only a few months before and after flowering in July. To truly appreciate the plant life of Soldiers Delight, you really need to get down on hands and knees.

Just before the trail enters the treeline under high tension lines, a collection of blackened tree stumps is visible to the left. In an effort to reverse the incursion of Virginia pines onto the grasslands, volunteers and staff at Soldiers Delight cut these scrubby trees. In addition, the grasslands are burned in late fall. These controlled burns kill young pines and recycle nutrients from dormant grasses; research from midwestern prairies indicate that fire is not only natural but necessary to maintain the health and biological diversity of such grasslands. Eventually, more than 1,000 acres at Soldiers Delight will be restored to their historic appearance as prairies.

The trail continues under the power lines, through a forest of stunted oaks, and eventually reaches Deer Park Road. At this point, follow the white blazes to the right, the trail paralleling the road. At the gravel parking lot, known as "the Overlook," you may extend your hike for another almost three miles (described below) by crossing Deer Park Road, or you may continue on the Serpentine Trail as it returns to the parking lot at the Visitor Center.

To complete the Serpentine Trail loop, continue on the white-blazed trail. Paralleling Deer Park Road but in the forest, this trail provides safe passage from speeding traffic. At an old dirt road, turn right; the Visitor Center is visible in the distance. The next 200 yards of trail traverse a landscape that has been actively managed for more than two decades. Pines have been removed and grasslands burned at least twice in this period. As a result, wildflowers are especially showy and diverse. September may be the best time to visit. Among the more common species you may see are Gray's goldenrod (the yellow spike) and grass-leaved blazing star (the purple spike). Both are frequently seen at Soldiers Delight but unusual elsewhere in Maryland. In September, look for sandplain gerardia along the edge of the trail. These pink, funnel-shaped flowers are modest but beautiful and are known from only a few other sites along the East Coast. The trail reaches the Visitor Center after about a quarter mile, completing the 2.2-mile circuit.

East Side Trails

Trails on the east side of Deer Park Road are blazed with three colors: red, orange, and yellow. However, these are not three distinct trails; they actually overlap. The shortest circuit, 1.4 miles, is blazed in red and is called the Choate Mine Trail. A longer circuit, 2.0 miles, picks up in the middle of the red trail, is marked with orange blazes, and is called the Red Run Trail. Finally, an extension of the orange trail is blazed in yellow (2.9 miles total) and is called the Dolfield Trail. If all this seems confusing, consult the map.

Begin your walk from the Overlook parking lot on Deer Park Road. There is usually ample parking available here, and there is overflow parking on the opposite side of the road, but there are no restrooms or potable water. There are excellent views of the rolling Piedmont countryside to the west from the Overlook, and this may be the best place near Baltimore to watch the sun set at day's end.

From the Overlook, cross Deer Park Road with care and walk north along the road shoulder for about 100 yards. The trailhead is marked with red blazes and leads directly into the pine forest.

Virtually all the pines at Soldiers Delight are Virginia pines (also known as scrub pines) and are less than thirty feet tall. They are limited in growth by the thin, dry soils, which are poor in several essential nutrients, especially nitrogen. The soils here are usually only a few inches thick, and may even be nonexistent in some places. Other plants that grow in the forest at Soldiers Delight are also adapted to dry conditions. These include post oaks, blackjack oaks, greenbrier, blueberries, and several kinds of mosses and lichens.

After a few hundred yards, the trail emerges from the forest into a savanna, where clumps of trees are randomly scattered about a grassland. Many of the pine trees here have recently been removed as part of a long-term project to restore the serpentine grasslands. Soldiers Delight may be Maryland's most ambitious project in ecosystem restoration.

The first trail intersection is encountered at mile 0.7. The red trail bears right, returning to Deer Park Road after 1.4 miles. For a longer walk through more diverse scenery, continue straight ahead on the trail, now blazed in orange. The trail soon reaches a small branch of the headwaters of Red Run. Soils are richer here along the creek, and there is a lush growth of ferns and wildflowers. Shrubs and small trees include mountain laurel, dogwood, sassafras, and red maple. This is one of Soldiers Delight's most enchanting spots, especially in autumn or early on a dewy summer morning with the sun's rays slanting through the swirling mists.

The trail soon leaves the floodplain of Red Run, rising through an oak forest. Houses become visible to the left as the trail runs near and parallel to the park boundary. At mile 1.3 the trail turns right, away from the nearby townhouses. This orange-blazed trail returns directly to Deer Park Road after a total distance of 2.0 miles. To continue hiking farther, however, look to the left for a yellow-blazed trail originating from the orange trail within sight of the townhouses.

This yellow trail proceeds through an abandoned orchard and then a field of thick grasses, goldenrod, and other wildflowers. It crosses Sherwood Road and then enters an oak forest. At mile 1.8, within earshot of Dolfield Road, the trail turns sharply right and proceeds through a typical Soldiers Delight landscape of scattered grasslands, greenbrier thickets, and glades of scrub pine. At mile 2.5, a major trail intersection is reached.

At this intersection, the orange-blazed trail comes in from the right and the red-blazed trail comes in from directly ahead. Turn left to return to Deer Park Road; the trail is now blazed in red.

At mile 2.8, look for the Choate chromium mine on the left, surrounded by a fence. This is the best-preserved of many mines at Soldiers Delight (but is still not safe to enter). In the early 1800s, the serpentine rock of Soldiers Delight was mined, taken to Baltimore by wagon, and smelted to extract chromium. Isaac Tyson, the well-known Baltimore merchant, made a fortune off Soldiers Delight chromium until richer deposits were discovered elsewhere in the mid- to late 1800s. The Choate mine was briefly reopened during World War I, when foreign supplies of chromium were interrupted. The chromium mined at Soldiers Delight was used in paints and in the manufacture of steel.

The trail continues, arriving at Deer Park Road opposite the Overlook parking area after a total distance of 2.9 miles. If your car is parked at the Visitor Center, cross Deer Park Road and follow the white-blazed Serpentine Trail to the left.

Directions

From the Baltimore Beltway (I-695), take Route 26 (Liberty Road) west toward Randallstown. Go 4.9 miles. Turn right on Deer Park Road and follow for 2.2 miles to the entrance to the Visitor Center. The Overlook parking area is just a few hundred yards north of the Visitor Center entrance on Deer Park Road.

Other Outdoor Recreational Opportunities Nearby

The McKeldin area of Patapsco Valley State Park is about a twenty-minute drive to the south. It has a fine system of trails, for both hiking and mountain biking, and is described elsewhere in this book.

DEER TICKS AND LYME DISEASE

Of all the disagreeable pests that occasionally plague people in Maryland's outdoors, deer ticks are among the most unpleasant. Since the mid-1980s, an increasing percentage of deer ticks have been host to *Borrelia burgdorferi*, the infectious bacterial agent responsible for Lyme disease. Lyme disease is the most common vector-borne disease in the United States. About 30,000 cases are reported to the CDC annually, but that number is a significant underestimate, since many cases never get relayed to that agency. The number of reported cases in Maryland ranged from just under 1,000 to as many as 2,500 annually in the decade 2005–2014.

Lyme disease is a nasty illness characterized initially by swelling and pain in the joints, headache, fever, and especially fatigue. If the disease remains untreated, arthritislike symptoms often develop. In later stages, cardiac arrhythmia, partial paralysis, meningitis, and permanent disability may occur. About 70 percent of cases exhibit a characteristic "bulls-eye" inflammation at the site of the tick bite, but the other one-third of patients have no such obvious marks. Furthermore, laboratory tests are inconclusive until about six weeks post-infection, the period of time the body needs to develop a good antibody response. Together, these characteristics sometimes make diagnosis difficult. Treatment with a course of antibiotics is effective early in the progression of the disease, but it cannot always cure the infection and alleviate the symptoms if given later. About 20 percent of patients have persistent symptoms, known as "post-treatment Lyme disease syndrome." They usually get better, but it may take a long time with many courses of antibiotic treatment.

The intermediate vector between humans and bacteria is the deer tick, also sometimes known as the black-legged tick. This modest tick is about the size of a sesame seed, significantly smaller than the more common dog tick. However, adult deer ticks rarely bite and transmit the disease to humans; it is the even tinier nymphal stage that is usually involved. Even a fully engorged nymphal deer tick is only about the size of the head of a pin. For this reason, people sometimes never notice the tick bite that transmits Lyme disease.

A female deer tick lays eggs in the spring. These eggs later hatch into larvae, which most often feed on blood from the common deer mouse. In the spring of the second year, larvae molt into the nymphal stage. If the nymph is successful in obtaining a blood meal, usually from deer or humans, it molts into an adult in early fall. After it again attaches to a mammal, mating occurs. The male deer tick dies, and the female overwinters, laying eggs in the spring to begin the two-year cycle again. Although mice, deer, and humans are the most typical hosts, ticks will bite almost any mammal from which they can get blood.

People who spend much time in brushy or grassy areas usually have several ticks on them by the end of the day. The most common tick is the dog tick, a species that does not carry the Lyme disease bacterium (it may, however, carry the causative agent of Rocky Mountain spotted fever). Dog ticks are larger; females have a large white dot on their backs, and males have white, wormlike markings. In addition to being less common, not all deer ticks are infected with the Lyme disease–causing bacterium. Furthermore, a deer tick must be attached for at least twenty-four hours before the bacteria is transmitted.

There are a few precautions that may lower your risk of getting bitten by a deer tick. Wear tightly woven, light-colored clothes so that you can easily see ticks, and tuck cuffs into your socks. Check your skin every time you return from the field. Nevertheless, the small size of nymphal ticks makes them easy to miss, so all of these measures are mostly of only psychological benefit. Stay out of woods, brushy areas, and tall grass, especially from midsummer through first frost. Spraying your shoes, socks, and pants with an insect repellent containing DEET may be helpful. The best advice is to be aware of Lyme disease symptoms and get immediate medical attention if such symptoms arise.

Gunpowder South Trail

County: Baltimore

Distance: 4.2 miles as described; out-and-back hike

Difficulty: Moderate. Hilly; rocky terrain

Dogs: Permitted on leash

Why It's Special: A narrow river valley with exceptionally clear, cold water hosting central Maryland's best trout fishery

More Information: Gunpowder Falls State Park, http://dnr.maryland.gov /publiclands/pages/central/gunpowder.aspx, (410) 592-2897

Street Address: None available for trailhead

GPS Coordinates: 39.611442, 76.682840 (Masemore Road trailhead)

The Big Gunpowder River is one of the most beautiful natural areas in Maryland. By virtue of this scenic character, it is also one of the best outdoor recreational sites. Arising from many small springs and seeps in the farmlands of northern Baltimore and Carroll Counties, the river flows through more than forty miles of protected parkland on its way to tidewater. Developed paths and primitive trails follow most of its length. Several stretches of river, both tidal and flowing, are suitable for canoeing and kayaking. As a greenway and corridor for wildlife, it skirts the development of Baltimore City and connects the Chesapeake Bay estuary with a variety of upland areas.

Much of the land bordering the Big Gunpowder River is preserved as Gunpowder Falls State Park. The park maintains a number of primitive trails for walking. One section, however, is so scenically outstanding as to warrant special mention, and it is described here. Running upstream from Masemore Road to the base of Prettyboy Dam is a narrow trail through a constricted valley, rich in thick vegetation and rocky outcrops. Alongside the trail, the river sparkles over

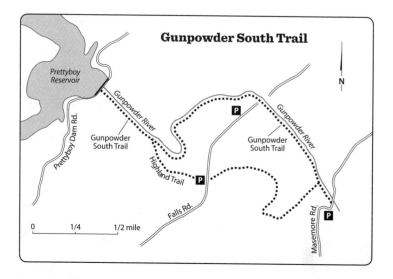

shallow riffles, dances through rocky chutes, and pours over steep drops into mysterious green pools. The overall impression is typical of a stream in far western Garrett County. In fact, this may well be the prettiest section of stream valley east of the mountains.

This hike of just over four miles round trip has one steep hill and a section where scrambling over and among rocks is necessary. Although not an easy trail, it is well worthwhile, and older children will enjoy the challenges of the hike.

Trip Description

Begin your hike from the small parking lot where Masemore Road crosses the Big Gunpowder Falls. There is room for about twenty cars, but there are no other facilities. This lot is heavily used by fly fishermen and paddlers, but only rarely is the available parking all full. Note that no parking is allowed near Prettyboy Dam at the far end of the trail.

Leaving the parking lot, walk upstream on the same (west) side of the river. For the next 0.7 miles, the Gunpowder South Trail, blazed in white, stays within steps of the Gunpowder. The river is usually quite shallow and moves slowly as it flows over tiny ledges and rock gardens. There are fine wildflowers along the riverbanks throughout the growing season, and frogs often plop into the water just ahead of your footfall. Overall, the scene is more pastoral than wild, in contrast to what lies ahead.

After a bit more than a half mile, cross Falls Road at a remote one-lane bridge that affords lovely views of the river and its well-shaded valley. After enjoying the scenery, continue on the Gunpowder South Trail in an upstream direction. Within 100 yards, a cliff extends to the river's edge, forcing the trail up and over this obstacle. Climbing steeply over jumbled rocks for about 50 feet, the trail crests at a knife-edge ridge and then drops equally steeply back to river level. This rocky barrier is the most difficult section of the trail.

The Big Gunpowder River here flows through a narrow, steep-sided valley. The hard, erosion-resistant mica schist rock has forced the river to wind its way through faults and cracks, creating a series of closely spaced, bouldery rapids. Small deep pools of flowing water are interspersed and invite a cooling dip on hot days. Be forewarned, however. Since the water comes out of the depths of Prettyboy Reservoir just upstream, it is bone-chillingly cold, even in summer. The trail through this rocky section is very broken, winding atop and between boulders and over twisted roots. Take your time and use care in making your way over this stretch of trail.

The V-shaped gorge through which you are walking has no room for a floodplain, so the big old trees shading the river are those adapted to rocky, cool hillsides. There are river birch with peeling, patchy bark; cherries; a few tulip poplars growing in patches of richer soil; and the ubiquitous oaks scattered throughout. At the steepest and rockiest sites, there are often a few hemlocks, trees typically found along streams and rivers in the western, colder parts of Maryland. This trail runs along the south bank of the Gunpowder, and so its northern exposure means that it gets much less sun in all seasons than the drier, exposed slopes on the opposite shore. An understory rich in mountain laurel, dogwood, spicebush, and witch hazel completes the list of important trees. Displays of early spring wildflowers like hepatica, bloodroot, spring beauty, and rue anemone are very fine in patches of rich woodland soil throughout the valley. By late summer and into fall, several species of petite woodland goldenrods and asters brighten the forest.

After about a third of a mile, the river's gradient relents, and rapids give way to gravelly shallows. Between here and Prettyboy Dam at least one beaver dam spans the river. Trees along the bank have been girdled and gnawed, and beaver tracks are sometimes evident in snow or mud. Beaver had been trapped out in Maryland for well over a hundred years when the Department of Natural Resources decided to reintroduce this charismatic fur-bearer in the 1950s. This stretch of the Gunpowder was the first place where beaver were reintroduced; they have since prospered and spread throughout the watershed. Today most stretches of river in Maryland have been recolonized by beaver.

The path soon heads uphill away from the water as the mountainside at river level becomes too steep for the trail; this point is marked by a blue wooden arrow labeled "Gunpowder South Trail." Although the path is narrow, there is good footing, and the higher elevation gives a nice view of the valley where the river makes a sharp bend. After a few hundred yards, this sidehill trail drops back to water level and runs straight for about a half mile. The imposing edifice of Prettyboy Dam soon dominates the narrow valley. On hot summer days, the little dell at the base of the dam may be the coolest place in Maryland, as the chill outflow air conditions the gorge.

After enjoying a rest at trail's end, begin your return via the same route. In just more than a half mile, turn right on the pink-blazed Highland Trail. It's a hilly trail with several tiny stream crossings, but this route gives you a change in scenery as it traverses the hills of Gunpowder Falls State Park. The trail crosses Falls Road near some power lines atop the ridge and then drops steadily to river level. Turn right on the Gunpowder South Trail; the Masemore Road trailhead is just downstream.

Although the superb scenery makes hiking this section of Gunpowder Falls State Park extremely rewarding, most of the visitors you will see are not hikers but anglers. Quite simply, this stretch of the Gunpowder River has some of the best trout fishing in Maryland, and indeed in the eastern United States. A survey in 2007 yielded more than 160 pounds of trout per acre and more than 4,300 trout per mile (in the first mile below the dam). In large measure, this superb fishery is due to restoration of minimum flows from Prettyboy Dam, negotiated by the Maryland chapter of Trout Unlimited and the Maryland Department of Natural Resources. Before the mid-1980s, there was excellent habitat for a trout fishery, but lack of water prevented the trout population from reaching its full potential. It is amazing that a simple management step like maintaining minimum flows in the river could have such a remarkable effect on the ecological community. Fishing is catch and release only and of course requires a license.

Directions

From the Baltimore Beltway (I-695), take I-83 north to Mt. Carmel Road, Route 137. Turn left. Continue on Route 137 for 1.8 miles; turn right on Masemore Road and follow it to the river and trailhead parking area.

Other Outdoor Recreational Opportunities Nearby

The Gunpowder South and Gunpowder North Trails continue downstream from Masemore Road for about five more miles. Many hiking trails surround Prettyboy Reservoir. Canoeing and kayaking on the Big Gunpowder River downstream from this section is superb when there is at least 100 cubic feet per second (cfs) of water flowing in the river (check the Parkton water gauge at https://waterdata.usgs .gov/md).

SALAMANDERS, FROGS, AND LOCALIZED EXTINCTIONS

Amphibians like salamanders and frogs play a surprisingly significant role in many ecosystems. For example, amphibian biomass often exceeds that of all other vertebrates combined in moist, mature forests. Although poorly studied and rarely considered in environmental assessments, amphibians make good bioindicators of changes in habitat quality because of their water- and air-permeable skin and their position high on the food chain.

Scientists who study amphibians assembled for the first time in 1990, and they were surprised to find that there were many reports of mortality and extinctions from all over the globe. It seemed that in the previous decade many populations of frogs and salamanders had declined or disappeared. Although local problems could account for some of the declines, others occurred in pristine and protected areas as diverse as national parks in California, Costa Rica, and Australia. Were these amphibians the first signal of some global, as yet unrealized, environmental problem?

Maybe. Scientists continue to collect data in the field that show declines and localized extinctions. Nevertheless, dismay has been tempered by a new understanding and appreciation of the population dynamics of amphibians.

For example, one group of scientists has been studying three species of salamander and one of frog in a South Carolina

(continued)

seasonal pond since 1979. They reported that population sizes varied significantly from year to year. For example, marbled salamanders showed a high of about 2,600 females in 1986 but a low of 3 in 1981. Tiger salamanders and chorus frogs each went locally extinct during the study, but each time their numbers rebounded in later years. Recruitment (survival of a new generation to metamorphosis) varied even more widely, by over five orders of magnitude.

The causative agent of these fluctuations was water. These amphibians breed in seasonal ponds that accumulate rainfall in the late autumn and winter and dry up completely in the summer. Wet years typically led to large populations and good recruitment, whereas dry years had the opposite effect. Thus the length of time over which water persisted in the pond was correlated with population size. Having evolved over millions of years with these episodic variations, amphibians have adapted to these "boom or bust" cycles.

When examining animals like amphibians, it is important to consider not only dramatic changes in the size of a population over time but also the context of their spatial arrangement Amphibian breeding sites are typically spread widely over suitable landscape; in dry years each site may be disjunct, whereas wet years may connect them with corridors of habitat suitable for migration. Thus a reproductive failure at one site may be offset by a wildly successful year elsewhere that provides excess animals for migration and colonization. Viewed over time and space, then, localized populations may fluctuate widely, winking in and out of existence like the flashing lights on a Christmas tree. This "metapopulation" theory may be helpful in understanding patterns of distribution and abundance among amphibians and other species.

Widespread variation in amphibian populations seems to be the norm, and observers who look at only one or two years of census data from a single location can come to erroneous conclusions regarding the rarity of salamander and frog species. This cautionary tale illustrates the importance of long-term scientific studies (and the money necessary to fund such research) in the examination of our natural heritage.

Patapsco Valley State Park: McKeldin Area

County: Carroll

Distance: 4.0 miles as described; circuit hike

Difficulty: Moderate. Hilly; rocky terrain

Dogs: Permitted on leash

Why It's Special: A beautiful Piedmont river valley with mature trees, a sparkling river, and lovely views

More Information: Patapsco Valley State Park, http://dnr.maryland.gov /publiclands/Pages/central/patapsco.aspx, (410) 461-5005

Street Address: 11676 Marriottsville Road, Marriottsville, Maryland 21104

GPS Coordinates: 39.358725, 76.889824 (contact station near trailhead)

As a linear, river valley park, Patapsco Valley State Park stretches more than forty miles from the river's upper reaches near Woodbine to tidewater at Baltimore Harbor. Never very wide, and interrupted by gaps where development reaches down to the water's edge, Patapsco Valley State Park still has some very pretty scenery in surprisingly pristine surroundings. One of the nicest sections of Patapsco is the McKeldin area, found near Marriottsville in Carroll County. Here, rolling hills and forested uplands lie in the fork of the river's north and south branches. Wildlife is abundant, trails are wide and well maintained, and visitor use is not heavy. All in all, it is a pleasant place to walk at any time of the year.

The trail described here is four miles in length. There are two hills and several other places where the trail is rocky and irregular, but the trail is not especially difficult. In the last few years, the McKeldin area has become popular with mountain bikers, so stay alert while on the trail. When snow covers the trails in winter, cross-country skiers test their skills against the curving, usually gentle downhills.

Trip Description

Begin your walk from the parking lot just beyond the contact station. A wheelchair-accessible bathroom is located here, as are picnic tables and water. To reach the start of the Switchback Trail, return to the contact station and follow the entrance road downhill. The trailhead is prominently marked with a wooden trail sign within 50 yards of the contact station. White blazes delineate the Switchback Trail over the next four miles.

The Switchback Trail belies its name at first, running straight through the ridgetop forest. To the right, mountain laurel fills the understory of this dry hillside; in late May, the flowers create a profusion of blooms reminiscent of snow. In keeping with the xeric nature of the soil, chestnut oaks form the canopy, although several other species typical of the more mesic part of the soil moisture scale are found here as well.

After about a third of a mile, the trail begins to drop steeply in a series of sharp turns, incising its way through the hillside. This area was once a flagstone mine, and the spoil piles still exist. Note the chunks of rock; they glitter in the sun. Mica is a major component of this metamorphosed quartzite. In places, thin plates of mica can be found that are transparent when peeled away into sheets.

The trail reaches the bottom of the hill and emerges onto the floodplain of the South Branch of the Patapsco. Follow the trail left through grassy and shrubby openings in the sycamore and locust woods. As the trail rises off the floodplain, take the right fork at a junction, bearing downhill toward the river. Here, closer to water, silver maples dominate, but the feeling of openness still persists. Occasional floods rising onto this bottomland dump sediment around the roots of resident trees and shrubs, killing many of them and resetting the clock of succession. The trail runs along the edge of the slow-moving river; look here for beaver, ducks, woodpeckers, kingfishers, and even the occasional great blue heron.

The trail soon leads up the side of a hill, emerging on top at a paved park road. Turn right on what is now the McKeldin Rapids Trail and

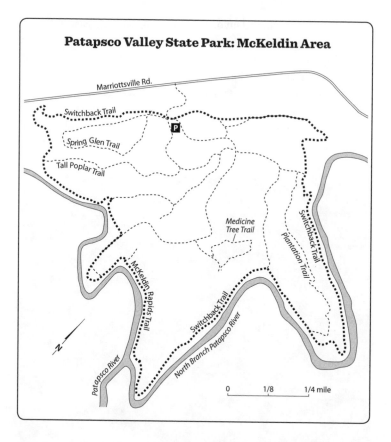

Patapsco Valley State Park: McKeldin Area

Marriottsville Rd.

Switchback Trail

P

Spring Glen Trail

Tall Poplar Trail

Medicine
Tree Trail

Switchback Trail

Plantation Trail

McKeldin Rapids Trail

Switchback Trail

North Branch Patapsco River

Patapsco River

N

0   1/8   1/4 mile

follow the road past picnic tables to its terminus. Continue downhill on the paved trail to the falls overlook. Here the South Branch of the Patapsco drops ten feet or so over a series of ledges into a wide pool, and the shaded dell forms a pretty scene.

At the downstream end of the falls viewing area, walk past an opening in the fence and scramble steeply downhill over exposed rocks. The gravel beach at the bottom is a popular sunbathing spot, but swimming is prohibited. The trail bears left, following a similar bend in the river. After a quarter mile, the river makes another 90° turn, this time to the right. There is a trail intersection here; you should follow the river, again on a rocky trail, to a hillside of exposed rock. Scoured of vegetation by storms, the gneiss that forms this outcrop is among the oldest rock in the Maryland Piedmont. Note how soil has accumulated in crevices and sheltered areas, allowing small plants to gain a foothold. Out on the bare rock, only mosses grow, low hardy cushions clinging to a precarious existence. The footing on these sloping rocks is usually slippery, especially if they are wet or icy; use care in crossing them.

The trail picks up on the far side of this rock outcrop, and the difficult parts are now behind you. Follow the narrow, sandy trail along the river for another quarter mile. Multiflora rose planted along here ensures birdlife in all seasons, and it is important as both food and

shelter in the winter, when the south-facing slopes and shielded river valley give protection to chickadees, titmice, cardinals, and other birds of brushy areas.

At the confluence of the North and South Branches, the McKeldin Rapids Trail now rejoins the Switchback Trail. Follow the footpath that ascends the North Branch of the Patapsco, paralleling the streambed. Water rarely flows in this arm of the Patapsco, since Liberty Dam is only about two miles upstream and rarely releases water. The result is a mostly dry slough. Nevertheless, pockets of rainwater persist into the summer, and this is a good place to surprise wood ducks and deer.

The trail traverses a fairly wide floodplain, with rich soils sponsoring a verdant undergrowth of shrubs and herbs. In spring, violets, bloodroot, spring beauties, and jack-in-the-pulpits bloom along the trail's edge. By summer, the pace of blooming slows, but such lesser-known forest herbs as agrimony, avens, crowfoot, enchanter's nightshade, and galinsoga flower modestly. Asters and goldenrods replace them by late summer and into fall. Spicebush, with yellow flowers and red fruits, is the most common shrub.

Over the next mile, as measured from the junction of the two forks of the Patapsco, two arms of the red-blazed Plantation Trail branch off, heading uphill. Stay with the Switchback Trail, along the river, for the best scenery. After a hairpin turn, the trail now heads due north through an increasingly constricted floodplain. Maidenhair ferns grow abundantly on this shady, rocky hillside, as do hepatica, bloodroot, and other early spring wildflowers. Unfortunately, so does wavyleaf basketgrass, an invasive ground cover native to Europe and Asia first discovered here in 1996. Although the park has tried to eradicate this plant with herbicidal sprays, it seems to return annually and spread a bit more each year.

The Switchback Trail reaches a point where rocky bluffs block farther passage upriver. The trail climbs steeply for 100 feet of elevation change to near the top of the ridge; take your time and watch your foot placement so as to minimize soil erosion on this unmaintained portion of the trail. Bear right, again following the white blazes of the Switchback Trail. A disconcerting aspect of this section of the park is the near-constant sound of gunfire; a firing range is located just outside the boundaries of the park on nearby Marriottsville Road. After another quarter mile, the trail rises yet again to a paved park road, picnic shelter, and restroom. When leaves are off the trees, there are distant views of Liberty Dam from an overlook.

Continue along the paved road, passing several more picnic pavilions, eventually reaching your car and completing this 4.0-mile circuit.

Directions

From the Baltimore Beltway (I-695), take I-70 west for 8 miles. Turn right (north) on Marriottsville Road. Continue for 4 miles to the park entrance on the right.

Other Outdoor Recreational Opportunities Nearby

Soldiers Delight Natural Environmental Area is located about a twenty-minute drive from the McKeldin area of Patapsco Valley State Park. It is described elsewhere in this book.

SEEING THE FOREST FOR THE TREES

When the first colonists landed in Maryland, much of the state was covered with mature forest. And Maryland's forests, in turn, were only a small part of the eastern forest that stretched over the entire continent westward to where the tallgrass prairie took over. Only in those few areas where the soil would not support trees were there significant natural breaks in this sea of chlorophyll. Native Americans also had an impact; by setting fires in the dry season, they created early successional habitats where hunting for game birds, rabbit, and deer was greatly improved.

Since the early 1600s, we humans have eradicated almost every acre of the original native forest in Maryland through clearing of land for agriculture, the harvesting of forest products, and the creation of roads, housing, and industry. Of course, trees are a naturally renewable resource, and they have grown back over time. Today, the Maryland landscape is a patchwork of tree stands of varying ages that cover about 60 percent of the state. As positive as this statistic sounds, it belies two significant facts. First, the rate of forest land loss, mostly to development, is higher in Maryland than in any other state in the east. Second, the nature of today's forests, in terms of ecology and species diversity, is remarkably different than that of the virgin forest.

Trees are the ecological dominants in the forest. That is, they are large and conspicuous and play an important role in forest ecology. For this reason, there is a tendency to look at forests as assemblages of trees. For example, the forest products industry defines a tree as being mature when the rate at which it accumulates wood tissue reaches a maximum. Although this age varies from species to species, it is only a small fraction of the life span of the tree. The pejorative term "overmature" is applied to older trees and is used as the justification for making the decision to begin logging. In fact, the forest ecosystem, of which the tree is but one part, continues to change and mature for at least another century.

For example, different species of trees dominate a typical Maryland Piedmont mesophytic forest at a hundred years than at fifty years. Ashes, elms, tulip poplars, locusts, red maples, and several types of oaks predominate at the earlier age; at a century, black and white oak are usually the most common species. Hickories reach the canopy even later.

Other changes occur that may be even more important. Among the leaves and branches, new species of insects appear. Although these species have been only poorly studied locally, an analogy to the biological diversity of tropical rain forest canopies may be instructive. When biologists first examined the insect life of those forests in the 1970s, they were astonished to find large numbers of species previously unknown to science, and a diversity and number that had never been even contemplated. Do such secrets remain hidden even today in Maryland forests?

Not all of a forest is above ground. Organisms important to the functioning of a forest ecosystem are found in the soil; without them, trees could not live. The top few inches of soil in a forest play an essential role in the nutrient cycles of the forest. Over time, the soil of a forest becomes increasingly enriched in organic

(continued)

matter as generations of leaves and insects decay. This process in turn conserves soil moisture and humidity, further improving soil conditions. Obscure organisms like bacteria, fungi, and tiny soil arthropods increase in number and diversity. They play a vital role as decomposers, recycling nutrients through the ecosystem.

Both on the surface and farther down in the soil, changes in the rhizosphere occur. Many plants have a mutually beneficial relationship between their roots and soil fungi. Typically the plant provides sugars for food, and possibly even some secreted protective chemicals, while the fungi assist the plant in the uptake of water and nutrients. In some cases, the association is so tight that the point where the plant ends and the fungus begins cannot be discerned even with the use of a microscope. Although the existence of these interactions is a known fact, the number and kinds of them and their role in the functioning of the forest ecosystem are as yet poorly understood.

The fungi associated with tree roots may be a bioindicator of the health of our forests. For example, if trees lose their associated fungi, they become less resistant to stress, including drought and cold. In Europe, where some forests have been dying since the late 1970s (probably because of air pollution), changes in forest fungi were noted even earlier. A rigorous survey of fungal species in marked, thousand- square-meter plots in Holland showed a decline from thirty-seven species in about 1970 to only twelve in 1990.

Thus a forest is more than just trees. It includes the herbaceous flora, a variety of birds, reptiles, amphibians, insects, and any number of tiny, obscure soil organisms. All are important to the proper functioning of the ecological community. So when trees are cut down, more than just wood is harvested; the entire ecosystem is disrupted. Unable to exist in the sun-blasted, erosion-rutted, wind-scarred soil, most of the life forms migrate or die. Nutrients are lost; soil moisture evaporates. And although the trees will grow back in about fifty years, the forest will not mature (in terms of its biological diversity and ecological functioning) for at least another century.

Hemlock Gorge Trail

County: Baltimore

Distance: 3.5 miles as described; circuit hike

Difficulty: Moderate. Hilly, with a narrow, rocky trail for the first mile

Dogs: Permitted on leash

Why It's Special: A steep-sided, clear-flowing creek in a vale surrounded by hemlock trees, reminiscent of western Maryland

More Information: Baltimore City Department of Public Works, Reservoir Natural Resources Section, http://publicworks.baltimorecity.gov/reservoirs

Street Address: Not available for trailhead

GPS Coordinates: 39.689279, 76.780454 (trailhead)

The forest primeval: shafts of sunlight slant through the branches of giant hemlocks, illuminating the swirling mists above the river. The water slips over rocks with hardly a sound, carrying the crimson leaf of a maple toward the sea. The morning quiet is broken only by the rattle of a kingfisher sweeping up the river, a small fish clasped tightly in her bill. There is no evidence of humankind, and the scene is at once peaceful and timeless. Every hiker wants to find such a special place, where beauty and solitude promote contemplation and serenity.

Such a place exists, even in Baltimore County. Hemlock Gorge, on the Big Gunpowder River upstream of Prettyboy Reservoir, is a tiny slice of Appalachia far from the mountains. Deeply incised into the surrounding landscape, the rocky gorge of the Gunpowder is lined by the trail's namesake hemlock trees, some of which are hundreds of years old. Given the scenic beauty of this trail, it is surprising how lightly it is used. When you visit such a pristine surrounding, be sure to haul out any trash you create; and if others have not been as respectful, you might take their debris as well. Minimize your impact on the fragile soils by staying on the trail and avoiding slopes where erosion is likely. The greatest threat to beautiful places like Hemlock Gorge is that they will be loved to death by too many of us.

Hemlock Gorge is owned by the City of Baltimore and is part of the Prettyboy Reservoir watershed lands. However, the City has no information about Hemlock Gorge in any form accessible to the public.

Trip Description

After parking along the shoulder of Gunpowder Road just beyond the bridge, walk down the wide grassy shoulder onto the floodplain. Within a few yards of the river, turn left (downstream) on a narrow footpath. For about 100 yards, this level path traverses a thick growth of riparian vegetation. There is a wide diversity of wildflowers in spring and again in late summer, and butterflies feed on the blossoms of tickseed sunflower and Joe-Pye weed. Especially common is a small tree, witch hazel, from which a popular liniment is extracted. Witch hazels are unique because they flower in the fall; their stringy yellow petals brighten the November forest after all the leaves have dropped.

The landscape and vegetation soon change. As the valley walls steepen and draw close to the water, hemlock trees begin to dominate, and they soon form a monoculture. Their dense shade precludes anything else from growing on the forest floor, so it is possible to see a long way through the forest. In addition, hemlocks self-prune, because the lower branches are shaded by upper ones, dropping their needles to enrich the duff on the forest floor. Indeed, the thick, spongy soil here is well-drained but holds in the underlying moisture, much as a mulch does. Soil compaction by heavy use affects soil structure and function, which is one reason walking off the trail can have a negative impact.

A few of the hemlocks are very large, with diameters of more than four feet. These giants are probably more than 300 years old. There are also hemlocks of lesser stature, and many thin young trees. Lumbering probably took place long ago in Hemlock Gorge, but at least not every tree was taken. Uphill from the trail, there are

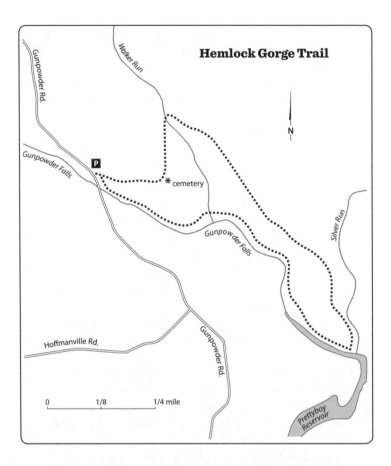

faint traces of several old wagon roads, probably used to haul out the trees or in mining.

The other obvious feature of the landscape is the many exposed rock outcrops. Although the rock itself is not green in color, it could easily be called greenstone, because mosses and lichens grow on every surface. These simple and commonplace plants are important to the ecology of any landscape. They secrete acids that, over time, slowly dissolve the rock into its constituent minerals, eventually creating soil for the growth of higher plants.

Within another hundred yards, the trail crosses a side stream. Beyond this point, the path becomes more difficult to walk, as you clamber over rocks and through a slalom course of trees. The river is now a few dozen feet lower than the trail, and the high perspective gives great views of the photogenic valley. The clear green water dances over rocks and around bends, pooling up into deep holes that invite a summertime swim. Observant hikers may discover two overhang caves that extend a few feet into the hillside. The surrounding rocks support small hemlocks that cling to cracks, seemingly without any soil to sustain them.

After about a mile and a half of travel, the valley widens just enough to create a small alluvial floodplain, and the adjacent slopes become less steep. The floodplain hosts a variety of spring wildflowers, including trout lilies, spring beauties, may apples, and skunk cabbage. Where a stream bars further progress, the trail bears left, soon entering the hardwood forest so typical of northern Baltimore County; hemlocks are only found on steep, shady slopes along precipitous creek valleys.

Where the trail becomes a fire road, turn left and ascend the hillside. Over the next three-quarters of a mile, the trail descends, crosses a stream, and rises to another ridge, where the Hoffman Gunpowder Burying Ground is found. Some of the gravestones here are more than two hundred years old and are in surprisingly good condition.

William Hoffman, a German immigrant, settled this area near the start of the Revolutionary War and constructed Maryland's first paper mill on the Gunpowder just downstream of Hemlock Gorge. The little cemetery is a peaceful place, but digging graves in the rocky soil must have been quite a task. After exploring the graveyard, follow the fire road downhill for a quarter mile to your car.

Directions

From the Baltimore Beltway (I-695), take I-83 north. Take exit 31, Middletown Road, to the west. Go 4.8 miles and turn left onto Beckleysville Road. After 0.3 miles, Beckleysville Road bears left; stay straight, on Cotter Road (presently lacking a road sign). Cotter Road eventually becomes Clipper Mill Road and crosses the Prettyboy Reservoir. Make the first right, onto Gunpowder Road. Go 0.7 miles and park on the wide road shoulder just beyond the bridge over the Gunpowder River.

Other Outdoor Recreational Opportunities Nearby

There is an extensive network of lightly used hiking trails on the Prettyboy Reservoir watershed lands located just downstream from Hemlock Gorge.

THE EXUBERANCE OF BEETLES

The eminent nineteenth-century evolutionary biologist Thomas H. Huxley was once asked by a clergyman what instruction might be taken from a study of natural history regarding God's plan for the universe. Huxley, tongue planted firmly in cheek, replied that God must have an inordinate fondness for beetles, given that there are so many of them. Indeed, there are more species of beetles in the order Coleoptera than there are species in any other order of plant or animal. This incredible diversification of a simple life form is one of the most striking and as yet unexplained patterns in nature.

Of the 1.5 million species of organisms now known to science, almost half are insects. There are more species of insects than of all other animals combined, and the total weight of all insects exceeds the weight of all other animals on earth, despite their diminutive size. Of the insect species, about half, or 300,000, are beetles. Scientists can only speculate on the reasons for this extensive diversification of the coleopterans. They probably evolved during the Mesozoic era about 200 million years ago; thus they are no more ancient than reptiles or amphibians. Beetles occupy virtually all terrestrial habitats; some are herbivores, some carnivores, and some detritivores.

Beetles are characterized by horny or leathery forewings that meet in a straight line down the back. These forewings are sometimes brightly colored and iridescent, enhancing beetles' appeal to collectors. Hindwings are membranous and are used in flight. Mouthparts, wonderfully diversified, are modified for chewing. Here in Maryland, beetles are common, especially in forested

(continued)

ecosystems. Among the most rare is the endangered northeastern beach tiger beetle.

It is this large variety of beetles that has led, in large part, to a reassessment of our view of biological diversity and the role of taxonomy in science. The identification and classification of organisms preoccupied science from the time of Linnaeus through the early twentieth century. Since then, technology and advances in inferential disciplines like biochemistry and molecular biology have shifted the emphasis (and funding) for the biological sciences. Today there are so few taxonomists that expertise in some obscure groups may reside in only a single researcher. Since the mid-1980s, however, there has been increased recognition that we need to discover, identify, and preserve our planet's living heritage before the inexorable spread of human culture causes the extinction of species as yet unknown.

This recognition came about from the study of beetles associated with tropical trees. In 1982, a Smithsonian Institution scientist sprayed an insecticidal fog into the canopy of a huge tropical rain forest tree and collected whatever fell on plastic sheets. To his astonishment, he identified over 1,200 species of beetles, many of them species new to science, and 162 of which were obligately associated with this one tree species. Extrapolating the data using a few simple assumptions, he estimated the total number of species on earth at as many as 30 million. Since only about 1.5 million species have currently been described, and since much of this diversity resides in fast-disappearing tropical ecosystems, scientists realized that much of our biological heritage might become extinct before we even knew it existed. Thus the exuberance of beetles has been the catalyst for a reanalysis of the significance of biological diversity on our planet.

Sugarloaf Mountain

County: Frederick
Distance: 5 miles as described; circuit hike
Difficulty: Moderate to strenuous. Very steep initial climb, then hilly
with rocks underfoot
Dogs: Permitted on leash
Why It's Special: A unique monadnock geological formation cloaked in a
maturing ridgetop forest with panoramic views of the countryside
More Information: Stronghold, Inc., www.sugarloafmd.com, (301) 874-2024
Street Address: 7901 Comus Road, Dickerson, Maryland 20842
GPS Coordinates: 39.252279, 77.392297 (entrance to Stronghold);
39.262248, 77.396803 (West View parking area)

The Maryland Piedmont, the area west of Baltimore and Washington and stretching to the Blue Ridge, is known for its gentle, ordered nature: scenic rolling hills, well-kept farms, peaceful shallow river valleys. Woodlots of old trees, preserved by longtime landowners, alternate in a patchwork with rich, deep-soiled agricultural fields. Wildlife is plentiful, even if it is the sort that has adapted to living in harmony with humans. The suburbs edge ever outward, year after year, but even today you can still go far enough "out" for it to seem rural. In the midst of this pastoral landscape, so much a product of the hand of humans, lies one incongruous mountain, towering wild and sentinel-like over the rolling countryside: Sugarloaf. Coming suddenly into view through your windshield, Sugarloaf Mountain, in southeastern Frederick County, is a surprise to all who travel here.

Sugarloaf is a monadnock: an isolated hill or mountain rising above an otherwise flat or gently rolling plain. The mountain itself is made of quartzite, a hard and erosion-resistant sandstone distinct from the rock of the surrounding Piedmont. Thus it has been less susceptible to weathering, standing about 700 feet above the rest of the countryside. The 570-million-year-old rock is similar to that found in the Blue Ridge a dozen miles or so to the west, but how the quartzite of Sugarloaf came to be here is not understood.

Unusual among parks and similar facilities, Sugarloaf is privately owned. No entrance fee is charged, no federal or state monies have ever been accepted, and it is always open (dawn to dusk). Managed by a nonprofit corporation, Sugarloaf is testimony to the vision and character of Gordon and Louise Strong. Recognizing the unique character of the site, this foresighted couple bought up most of the mountain and in 1946 transferred it to Stronghold, Inc., to manage. Sugarloaf was designated a National Natural Landmark in 1969.

The route described traverses much of the Sugarloaf massif and includes both its highest point and three other hilltops. The trails at Sugarloaf are surprisingly difficult, given that they are located in the normally gently rolling terrain of the Piedmont physiographic province. Expect some tough climbs on rocky trails. While the total distance for the suggested hike is five miles, shorter routes are possible for those with less time or energy. Most visitors to Sugarloaf climb one of the steep trails from the parking lots to the highest point, but while both choices are only a quarter mile each, they rise almost 400 feet in that short distance. Still, the views from the top are well worthwhile. For this reason, the route described begins with that steep climb; the remainder of the hike is on the blue-blazed Northern Peaks Trail.

Trip Description

Begin your walk from the West View parking area, reached by a winding one-lane paved road originating at the well-marked entrance to the Sugarloaf Mountain property. There are about fifty parking spaces at West View, two portable bathrooms, and several picnic tables. In the event all the parking spaces are taken, as often occurs on spring and fall weekends, parking is allowed as noted on the shoulder of the road.

The most direct route to the summit is the green-blazed trail, originating near the picnic shelter. The initial hundred yards rise pleasantly uphill on a well-constructed trail that often uses flat

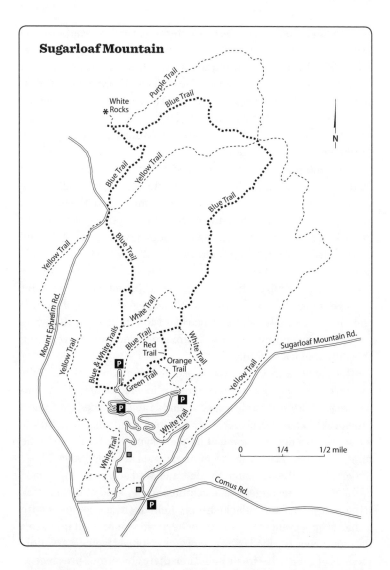

Sugarloaf Mountain

pieces of the local stone as steps. Alongside the trail are many boulders that have come to rest here after having fallen from the upper reaches of the peak. The rock that composes much of Sugarloaf is quartzite, a metamorphosed sandstone that is exceptionally hard and thus resistant to erosion. It is identical to the quartzite that tops the Blue Ridge just a short distance to the west, and suggests a common geological origin.

Cliffs soon appear, and the trail enters a gap in this escarpment on a series of more than one hundred concrete steps. Fortunately, there is a handrail to assist your climb, as this is a strenuous section for even the well-conditioned hiker. The stairs end near the summit, at an elevation of 1,282 feet, more than 700 feet above the surrounding countryside. The summit platform is fairly flat, about an acre in size, and has views to the west and north; the Potomac River is visible in the distance, as is the Blue Ridge.

After admiring the view, proceed downhill on the red-blazed trail for a quarter mile. Turn right on the Northern Peaks Trail; you'll be following its blue blazes for the remainder of the hike. Not only are there blue blazes painted on prominent trailside trees, but every half mile is designated by a wooden post set in the ground and painted with an alphanumeric symbol. Thus, the first one you'll see is B2; that means you are on the blue-blazed trail and are one mile from its origin at the West View parking lot. Coincidentally, B2 is very near the first of the "northern peaks"; at 1,071 feet, it is well below the high point at Sugarloaf Mountain, but still towers above the surrounding terrain. There are no views, however, from this fully wooded summit.

One particularly striking feature of the landscape at Sugarloaf is that virtually every boulder is covered in lichens. Lichens are a symbiotic association of an algal species and a fungal species; the fungus provides the alga with structure and protection against desiccation, while the alga donates some of its photosynthetic products to the fungus for growth. The most common lichen is a light green foliose lichen that is always rough to the touch and seems almost a part of the rock. Many larger rocks exhibit another kind of lichen, rock tripe. These leaf-like, blackish-grey lichens invest boulders with a shaggy appearance. Rock tripe lichens were once used to make a thin soup, clearly a food of last resort for colonists facing starvation. Lichens are sensitive to air pollution; their ubiquitous presence at Sugarloaf indicates good air quality at a surprisingly close distance to Washington, DC.

The trail continues northward in a rolling fashion, passing over another promontory before reaching a major trail junction at about mile 2.2. Here the yellow-blazed trail crosses the Northern Peaks Trail. The yellow-blazed trail is also open for mountain biking on selected days of the week between Memorial Day and Labor Day.

A third trail, marked with purple triangles, originates from this point; it follows the same general course as the Northern Peaks Trail, but at a somewhat lower elevation and extends the total hiking distance by an additional half mile.

Continue on the well-marked blue-blazed Northern Peaks Trail as it ascends rather steeply to yet another promontory at an elevation of 1,015 feet. Again, the summit is well forested, so there are no views. Fortunately, the overlook at White Rocks is just less than a mile ahead. There are actually two distinct west-facing lookouts, each from a jumble of steep-sided quartzite boulders that give fine views over the countryside more than 400 feet below. White Rocks is perhaps the best location on the Northern Peaks Trail for a rest and refreshment stop.

After enjoying the views, take the rocky trail downhill into an enclosed valley transected by Mt. Ephraim Road. It's a shady vale, and the only location on Sugarloaf Mountain with a perennial stream. There are richer soils here, and thus taller trees, wildflowers in spring, and several varieties of ferns. Turn left at the road, walk along it for about 100 yards, and look for the clearly marked trail post indicating where the trail returns to the forest. The remaining mile of trail is perhaps the most delightful segment of the Northern Peaks Trail, as it follows the tiny stream to its springhead and then traverses the west side of the property. Mountain laurels are common here and throughout much of the Sugarloaf forest; in late May the white blossoms of this small tree lend a beautiful and festive feeling to the woods. The final hundred yards of the Northern Peaks Trail rise steeply to the West View parking area and the completion of the circuit.

Directions

From Washington, DC, take I-270 north. From Baltimore, take I-70 west, then I-270 south. On I-270, take exit 22. Turn west on Route 109, Old Hundredth Road, and go 2.8 miles. Turn right on Comus Road. Go 2.4 miles to the well-marked entrance to the Sugarloaf Mountain property.

Other Outdoor Recreational Opportunities Nearby

Within a thirty-minute drive is the C&O Canal towpath, with excellent hiking and cycling possibilities. A short distance to the northeast is Montgomery County's Little Bennett Regional Park, with many miles of trails.

LICHENS

Lichens are enigmatic residents of the natural world we share. They are a paradox: familiar but often unnoticed, seemingly simple but actually complex, little appreciated but fascinating, often hardy but sometimes sensitive.

Many hikers have noted these curious structures on rocks and tree bark but pass by without a second thought. That's a shame, because lichens are marvelously diverse in shape, color, and texture, well worth a careful examination. They come in virtually every color of the rainbow (although admittedly most lichens found in Maryland forests tend toward drab hues of green, gray, and brown). In terms of structure, lichens can be fruiticose (branched), foliose (flat like the pages of a book), or crustose (flaky or crusty). Reproductive structures can look like tiny cups. But what sets a lichen apart from most living things is that it is a mutually beneficial association between a fungus and an alga. The algal cells perform photosynthesis, donating up to 80 percent of the sugars produced by that process to the fungus, while the fungus provides structure and some degree of protection against desiccation and predation. In this sense, both partners benefit, a relationship known as symbiosis. It's a successful relationship; by one estimate, about 6 percent of the Earth's surface is covered by lichens.

Lichens play a minor but important role in the biosphere. They are often the first kind of organism to colonize new and inhospitable habitats, like rock newly exposed by landslides or avalanches. Lichens secrete acids that chemically weather rock, releasing minerals for use by plants and generating cracks that provide a foothold and shelter for other living things. Lichens are often hardy to an extreme. In 2005, lichens were taken into space and exposed to its vacuum, extreme temperatures, and electromagnetic radiation. The lichens seemed unaffected, living and growing normally when returned to Earth. Despite this demonstrated hardiness, some lichens are quite sensitive to air pollution and can be used as living biosensors of air quality.

While about 90 percent of lichens have algae as the photobiont, the remainder partner with cyanobacteria, photosynthetic organisms more closely related to nonphotosynthetic bacteria than green algae (which are part of the plant kingdom). Cyanobacteria are capable of taking nitrogen from the atmosphere and converting it to forms usable by fungi and higher plants to enhance their growth. And some lichens have *both* green algae and cyanobacteria. An example is rock tripe, a large, conspicuous foliose lichen adorning many rocks in the Maryland mountains.

While this symbiotic relationship between algae or cyanobacteria and fungi has been known to science for more than 150 years, only in 2016 was it discovered that some lichens actually contain two kinds of fungi, not one. Embedded in the outer cortex of some lichens are basidomycete yeast cells that produce chemicals likely to deter feeding by predators and ward off invasion by bacteria. Although these yeast cells were visible in the microscope, scientists had never realized they were different from the well-known ascidomycete fungal cells that characterize lichens. Only when researchers found that some genes being expressed were not from the alga or primary fungus did they realize that there was a second fungal partner, a previously unknown species of yeast from an obscure, early-evolving group of basidiomycetes. This observation explained why lichens had never been successfully made in the laboratory by mixing known algal and fungal partners together.

Lichens have been called "self-contained miniature ecosystems" and "fungi that have discovered agriculture." Both of these monikers are memorable but are simplifications of the complexity that science is still discovering about this fascinating member of Maryland's, and our planet's, biological heritage.

The Appalachian Trail

Counties: Frederick, Washington
Distance: Pen Mar to Wolfsville Road: 10.0 miles
    Wolfsville Road to Route 40: 8.6 miles
    Route 40 to Washington Monument State Park: 3.5 miles
    Washington Monument State Park to Gapland Road: 8.8 miles
    Gapland Road to the Potomac River: 10.0 miles
Difficulty: Strenuous. Steep climbs at passes, relatively flat along ridges;
    rocky terrain
Dogs: Permitted on leash
Why It's Special: Scenic vistas; ridgetop forest
More Information: Appalachian Trail Conference, (304) 535-6331;
    South Mountain State Park, (301) 791-4767

The Appalachian Trail (AT) is the most famous walking trail in the world, and we are fortunate that a section of it traverses Maryland. Forty-one miles of the AT follow the crest of the Blue Ridge between Pen Mar and Harpers Ferry, providing the opportunity to hike or backpack through some fine mountain scenery punctuated by several dramatic overlooks. In addition, the trail passes through the site of a small but significant Civil War battle, South Mountain.

The AT runs more than 2,000 continuous miles between Springer Mountain, Georgia, and Mount Katahdin, Maine. It was the brainchild of Benton MacKaye, who in 1921 proposed linking a series of currently existing trails into a continuous network. It was an idea whose time had come; it was immediately accepted, and thousands of volunteers and Civilian Conservation Corps crews laid out and built the trail. Completed in 1937, the AT was named the nation's first "National Scenic Trail" in 1968. Federal and state

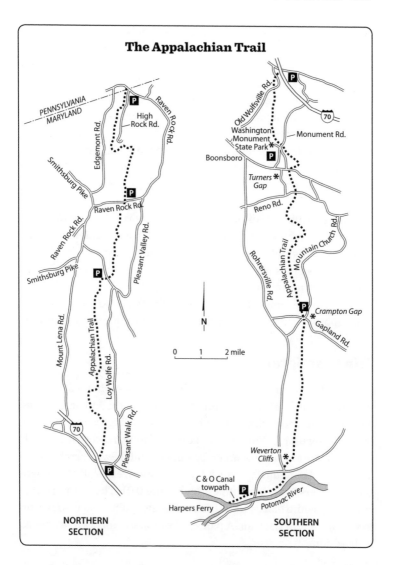

The Appalachian Trail

PENNSYLVANIA
MARYLAND

Edgemont Rd.

High
Rock Rd.

Raven Rock Rd.

Smithsburg Pike

Raven Rock Rd.

Raven Rock Rd.

Smithsburg Pike

Pleasant Valley Rd.

Mount Lena Rd.

Appalachian Trail

Loy Wolfe Rd.

Pleasant Walk Rd.

N

0   1   2 mile

Old Wolfsville Rd.

70

Washington
Monument
State Park *

Monument Rd.

Boonsboro

Turners *
Gap

Reno Rd.

Rohersville Rd.

Appalachian Trail

Mountain Church Rd.

Crampton Gap *

Gapland Rd.

Weverton
Cliffs *

C & O Canal
towpath

Harpers Ferry

Potomac River

**NORTHERN
SECTION**

**SOUTHERN
SECTION**

money has since been appropriated to buy the trail corridor and surrounding buffer lands, ensuring permanent protection for this national treasure.

Hiking the AT affords one the chance to connect with a much larger community of outdoorspeople, past and present, who have enjoyed and even been changed by their experiences on the trail. Each year, several thousand people set out to hike the entire trail, an adventure that takes a minimum of five months. Despite the hardships of cold and heat, biting insects, rain and mud, too little water and food, and the physical deterioration of the body that occurs after endless days of physical exertion, many "thru-hikers" report their experience to be the most significant period of personal growth of their lives. Many mention that friendships formed with other hikers along the way are deep and intense in a way that more casual relationships in the outside world can never be. The largest pulse of thru-hikers reaches Maryland between Memorial Day and Father's Day; a conversation with one of them is always interesting.

Although the AT is definitely a mountain trail, much of it is not excessively difficult hiking. Large segments run for several miles along the crest of the Blue Ridge with little change in elevation. Significant uphills and downhills tend to be clustered at the trailheads, where roads cross the escarpment at gaps and hollows. Judicious use of this guide or the excellent topographic map published by the Potomac Appalachian Trail Club will allow selection of a trail segment appropriate for the experience and fitness level of your group.

Trip Description

For the following trip descriptions, the AT has been divided into convenient sections for long day hikes or short overnight backpackers. The segments correspond to those road crossings where parking is readily available. For backpackers, be forewarned that cars left overnight are an obvious target for vandals and thieves; arrange for a drop-off and pick-up if possible. Mileages are given relative to where the AT enters Maryland at Pen Mar (mile 0.0). The entire trail is marked by white blazes, 2 × 6-inch rectangles painted at eye level on trees adjacent to the trail. A pair of blazes alerts hikers to a change in direction.

Pen Mar South to Wolfsville Road

This most northerly section of the AT in Maryland is perhaps the hilliest in the state. The trail crosses the Pennsylvania border into Maryland at the little town of Pen Mar. Once a vacation community for city dwellers who wanted to take the mountain air, Pen Mar features some beautifully kept, very large old houses. The trail runs fairly flat for 2.5 miles but then climbs steeply over what is basically a rock pile for more than 500 feet of elevation change to High Rock. A dramatic rock outcrop with fine views of the Hagerstown Valley to the southwest, High Rock is the premier hang glider launch site in Maryland. On any weekend with a decent breeze from the appropriate direction, pilots will launch themselves off the cliff in what is truly a leap of faith. Spiraling on thermals rising from the heating valleys, they can stay aloft for up to several hours and look down on miles of Maryland landscape.

To avoid the drudgery of the difficult slog to High Rock, day hikers can consider driving up High Rock Road and parking at the top (there is no overnight parking). The AT is accessed from here by a short, blue-blazed branch trail. From this point, the AT rises a further 250 feet in elevation to its highest point in Maryland, at just over 2,000 feet atop Quirauk Mountain. Over the next 2.5 miles, the trail dips almost 1,000 feet into pretty Raven Rock Hollow. Like many such coves in the Appalachian Mountains, richer, deeper soils accumulate here, and springheads and headwater streams make water available for plant growth. Trees grow taller, there is more diversity, and understory growth is more luxurious. After crossing Raven Rock Road, the trail climbs over Buzzard Knob and into Warner Gap, a narrow, shady dell where hemlocks are common. The last two and half miles in this section cover shallow hills.

Wolfsville Road South to Route 40

This section of the AT in Maryland is one of the easiest and has two striking overlooks that are a favorite day-hike destination. It is also quite popular as a moderately easy backpack trip, with a designated backcountry campsite and a reliable water source about halfway along the route.

The parking lot at Wolfsville Road is small but situated in a nice hemlock forest. The trail rises several hundred feet out of this shallow gap but then runs along the ridge with only small changes in elevation for the next six miles. This narrow ridge, known as South Mountain, is capped by quartzite, a hard, erosion-resistant rock. Together with Catoctin Mountain to the east, South Mountain was once the middle slopes of a much larger and higher peak. Over time, the action of water and wind eroded the softer rock that composed the bulk of this mountain so that what was once its center now lies at a lower elevation and forms the Middletown Valley.

Ridgetops are dry habitats for plant life, since springs and seeps typically emerge at lower elevations. Soils are thin and poor in nutrients. Under these harsh conditions, fewer plants can survive and thrive. Thus this ridge is dominated by chestnut oak, a tree so well adapted to dry, poor soils that in places it may be the only tree species present. Chestnut oaks are easy to recognize, with thick, furrowed bark and a wavy-edged leaf. Gypsy moths prefer oak, and so in the 1980s they made their first penetrations southward into Maryland along these ridges. Although some trees died from several consecutive years of defoliation, most remain healthy, and gypsy moths have probably not had any long-term effects on this forest.

Near the old Black Rock Hotel site at mile 14.8 is the Pogo Campground. It is one of the few places on the trail where springs emerge close to the ridgeline. Within another mile and after a short climb, a marked side trail leads to Annapolis Rock. This striking outcrop of quartzite gives a panoramic view of the valley below. It often catches the breeze, and so it is a cool place to rest on a hot day. Interstate 70 passes far below; Annapolis Rock and the nearby Black Rock are the boulder piles visible from the highway. A surprising amount of noise reaches these overlooks from the highway, testament to mankind's all-pervasive influence on the natural environment.

The trail south from Annapolis Rock runs flat for a short distance and then drops steeply downhill to Route 40 at mile 18.6. The most popular day hike on the Maryland section of the AT is an out-and-back route that begins at Route 40 and runs northward to the overlook at Annapolis Rock.

Route 40 South to Washington Monument State Park

This short segment is described separately because the state park is often a destination in itself and it is a relatively safe place to leave vehicles.

The AT leaves Route 40 and crosses Interstate 70 by a footbridge. Over the next 2.5 miles, a rolling but generally uphill hike leads to the base of Monument Knob. Here the trail rises steeply for 250 feet to a little pinnacle topped by the nation's first monument to George Washington. It's an ugly, jug-shaped structure of native stone, but there are nice views of the surrounding countryside from its top.

The monument is also Maryland's premier site for watching the annual fall migrations of hawks. As the days shorten, hawks and other predatory birds like ospreys and eagles begin drifting south for the winter. They congregate over several major flyways, one of which leads down the spine of mountains that includes the Blue Ridge. As prevailing winds strike these isolated ridges, updrafts are created that the birds can use to gain altitude. Spiraling upward on these invisible wind currents, hawks can conserve energy by gliding rather than having to flap. Once the updraft gives out, the birds drift southward to the next rising air current.

Two species of hawks dominate the autumn migrations. Broad-winged hawks are moderate-sized, soaring hawks characteristic of woodlands. On occasion, proper winds at peak migration will give rise to dramatic "boiling kettles" of several dozen birds soaring in tight circles within an updraft. Broadwing migration usually peaks in about the middle of September. During the first week in October, sharp-shinned hawks dominate. These small accipiters, not much larger than a blue jay, have pointed wings, a squared-off tail, and bright coloration around the head and chest. Sharpies are among the "fighter planes" of the bird world; feeding almost exclusively on songbirds taken on the wing, they are fast and highly maneuverable. Although broad-wings and sharpies are the two species most frequently seen from the monument, birders delight in spotting the rarities: merlins, goshawks, peregrines, and eagles.

A side trail connects the AT to the parking lots at the state park.

Washington Monument State Park South to Gapland Road

This section of the AT is another hilly one, with numerous climbs and descents. It is perhaps of greatest interest to those who enjoy visiting Civil War battle sites; they can traverse the land where the Battle of South Mountain was fought.

The AT drops steeply southward from the Washington Monument, rises a bit, and then begins a mile-long, shallow descent to Turners Gap. At less than 1,000 feet elevation, Turners Gap is the lowest Blue Ridge crossing, and it is about two miles in width. For backpackers, the Dahlgren campsite 100 yards south of the gap has running water, flushing toilets, and free hot showers, a luxury unimaginable to long distance hikers on the AT.

In mid-September 1862, the Army of Northern Virginia under General Robert E. Lee had advanced north into Maryland. It split into several groups and became dispersed over much of central

Maryland. About half of Lee's troops laid siege to Harpers Ferry in hopes of capturing that important Union garrison, with its abundant munitions and supplies. The rest encamped near Hagerstown, their flank guarded by the Blue Ridge and a light garrison of troops in Turners Gap and Crampton Gap.

The Union Army, under General George B. McClellan, was stationed east of the mountains, searching for the Confederates. By September 14, McClellan knew where Lee was, and he began marching up old Route 40 toward Turners Gap. Although the rebel army held the high ground, they were badly outnumbered, and the width of the gap made their position susceptible to a flanking maneuver. Fighting was fierce for most of the day, although the Union army got only a small portion of its troops into action. Confederate reinforcements arrived just in time, and by nightfall they still held their ground. After dark, the rebels withdrew, having achieved their strategic goal of slowing the Federal army. Harpers Ferry would soon fall, and both armies would gather at the nearby hamlet of Sharpsburg on September 17 for a battle that would change the course of American history: Antietam.

Only a series of roadside plaques marks the battle at Turners Gap. With the exception of the AT corridor, much of the site is privately owned, slipping quietly into history.

South of old Route 40 (now Route 40A), the AT continues mostly flat for two miles. It then climbs unrelentingly upward for more than a mile to Lambs Knoll and then drops slowly to Crampton Gap and Gapland Road at mile 30.9.

Gapland Road South to the Potomac River

Crampton Gap is another of the low passes through the Blue Ridge. Like Turners Gap to the north, it was the site of a Civil War battle on September 14, 1862. However, because this is a narrower defile, the fight was smaller and of less significance. A few roadside markers commemorate the battle.

Also at the Gapland Road trail crossing is an unusual monument. A large castlelike arch of stone was erected by Civil War correspondent Alfred Gath in the years after the war. It is the only known monument to war correspondents. The arch and the nearby graveyard lend an eerie presence to the old battlefield.

This section of trail is probably the easiest for hikers who want to get on the AT but are not sure of their capabilities. The trail rises gently out of Crampton Gap and then runs fairly flat for almost five miles. The only difficulty is the footing; the entire AT is extremely rocky, and care must be taken to avoid tripping or sliding.

At mile 36, the trail begins a long downhill stretch leading to the Potomac River. There are fine views of the river and the water gap at Harpers Ferry from Weverton Cliffs, the final overlook before the trail drops steeply to the river. Finally, the trail runs west for almost three flat miles along the C&O Canal towpath. This is a scenic section of the C&O Canal; the Potomac is often visible from the towpath as it rushes over a series of noisy rapids. Boulders stud the river, and big trees like sycamores and silver maples shade the river bank and towpath. Just opposite the town of Harpers Ferry, a footbridge spans the Potomac River and the trail leaves Maryland.

GYPSY MOTHS

The forests of Maryland have faced a variety of insults and threats since European colonization more than 350 years ago. Trees have been burned down; ripped up; sawed through; infected by fungi and bacteria; subjected to acid rain, ozone, and air pollution; and generally treated badly. Unfortunately, the 1980s added injury to insult with the arrival of gypsy moths. These small forest lepidopterans are exotics, a Eurasian species brought to the United States in 1869. They quickly escaped and have been munching their way through the eastern forest for more than a century.

The life cycle of gypsy moths is now familiar to most Marylanders; citizens have become intimately acquainted with this insect to a degree they never would have thought possible. Tiny caterpillars hatch out of tannish egg masses in mid-April and climb upward onto tree limbs. Leaves have just appeared, and the larvae eat the tender young foliage. As these larvae grow, they shed their outer skin, going through five molts for males and six for females. At maturity, the hairy caterpillars may be up to 2.5 inches long, and they are recognized by five pairs of dark blue spots followed by six pairs of brick red spots on the back. By mid-June, the larvae spin a cocoon and pupate for about two weeks.

(continued)

Adult moths hatch out; males are gray to brown, whereas females are off-white and flightless. Mating occurs within a few days of emergence, and after the eggs are laid the moths die quickly.

Heavy infestations of gypsy moths can have significant effects on forest trees. For example, the Savage River State Forest in Garrett County had about half its acreage defoliated in 2006 and 2007. Since 1980, about a million acres of Maryland forests, both public and private, have experienced gypsy moth–induced defoliations in at least one growing season. A healthy tree can usually survive one year of defoliation, but three consecutive years are often fatal. A hike along Maryland's Appalachian Trail reveals many such dead trees, trees that have succumbed to gypsy moths over the last few decades.

Fortunately, such acute damage usually occurs only at the leading edge of the expanding gypsy moth range; once gypsy moths have been established for a few years, the population often crashes dramatically. In large measure, this decline is due to the arrival of predators and parasites of gypsy moth caterpillars, although weather plays a significant (but unpredictable) role as well. For example, in the winter of 2015 more than a half-million acres were surveyed for gypsy moth egg cases. So few were found that the annual aerial spraying program (see below) was curtailed that year.

In response to public pressure in the 1980s, Maryland's Department of Agriculture instituted an aerial spraying program to control gypsy moth outbreaks. At present, the insecticide of choice is Dimilin, an effective chemical that interferes with the ability of a gypsy moth larva to molt. Dimilin has low toxicity to humans and other mammals and does not accumulate in the food chain. However, studies have shown that Dimilin persists in the environment for many months and affects a variety of nontarget organisms, including aquatic insects and crustaceans.

For this reason, Dimilin is never used near streams, rivers, or lakes. Instead, riparian forests are sprayed with *Bacillus thuringiensis* (Bt), a bacterium that produces a protein toxic to moths and butterflies. Although Bt has a more specific host range, its window of activity is smaller; it must be ingested at the second or third caterpillar growth stage, or instar.

The long-term implications of gypsy moths for our forests are now becoming clear, after several decades of living with this forest pest. Gypsy moths prefer oak leaves, and oak is the dominant forest tree throughout much of Maryland. It is conceivable that less palatable trees like tulip poplar may soon assume a more dominant role in the canopy. Less obviously, repeated spraying reduces populations of forest insects, especially butterflies and moths, with unknown effects on the ecology of the forest. What is certain is that gypsy moths will be with us for the foreseeable future and that we will have to learn to accept some background level of damage to trees in forests and around our homes.

Maryland Heights

County: Washington

Distance: 6.6 miles as described; circuit hike

Difficulty: Strenuous. Steep mountain hiking, some on an old dirt road but much on rocky trails

Dogs: Permitted on leash

Why It's Special: Some of the best views in Maryland, of three states, two major rivers, and a historic town, and passing through a well-preserved Civil War battlefield

More Information: Harpers Ferry National Historical Park, www.nps.gov /hafe/index.htm, (304) 535-6029.

Street Address: 171 Shoreline Drive, Harpers Ferry, WV 25425 (Cavalier Heights contact station); 554 Harpers Ferry Road, Knoxville, MD 21758 (Harpers Ferry Road trailhead)

GPS Coordinates: 39.316970, 77.756705 (Cavalier Heights contact station); 39.328771, 77.731216 (Harpers Ferry Road trailhead)

The passage of the Patowmac through the Blue Ridge is perhaps one of the most stupendous scenes in Nature. . . . The scene is worth a voyage across the Atlantic." So Thomas Jefferson described the area around Harpers Ferry, where the three states of Maryland, Virginia, and West Virginia converge. High hills, steep cliffs, and tumbling whitewater make for beautiful scenery, and few places in the mid-Atlantic states have witnessed as many events of historical significance. Harpers Ferry is a fine destination for a day in the outdoors.

Much of the lower town of Harpers Ferry is a National Historical Park, restored and operated by the National Park Service. The US Armory and Arsenal here was seized by abolitionist John Brown in 1859 in an incident widely considered the most important event

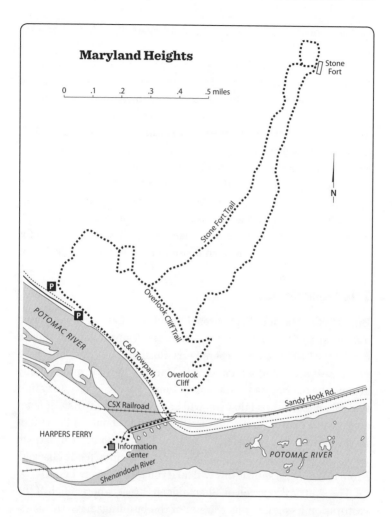

Maryland Heights

0 .1 .2 .3 .4 .5 miles

Stone Fort

Stone Fort Trail

Overlook Cliff Trail

N

POTOMAC RIVER

P

P

C&O Towpath

Overlook Cliff

Sandy Hook Rd.

CSX Railroad

HARPERS FERRY

Information Center

POTOMAC RIVER

Shenandoah River

presaging the Civil War. North and South exchanged control of the water gap many times between 1861 and 1865. Industry and commerce flourished both before and after the war, fueled by abundant water power, access to transportation systems (the C&O Canal and B&O Railroad) and surrounding rich farmland. Its location in the floodplain of both the Shenandoah and Potomac Rivers, however, made the town subject to devastating floods, and by the Depression, Harpers Ferry had become just another sleepy little mountain backwater. Tourism has now enlivened its fortunes, and the privately owned upper town is filled with curio shops, snack bars, and visitors. You'll no doubt want to visit Harpers Ferry before or after your walk.

The hike described here begins and ends in Harpers Ferry, West Virginia. After crossing the Potomac River on a footbridge and walking a short distance on the C&O Canal towpath, the trail climbs steeply to Maryland Heights, where there are spectacular views of three states, two major rivers, and one historic town. From this point, the trail climbs farther up the mountain, passing several Civil War–era cannon emplacements, eventually reaching the remains of a fort from the same era. This site was the location of a September 1862 battle that, although minor in terms of numbers of soldiers engaged, had strategic importance. The trail is strenuous, with about 1,000 feet of elevation change, but the rewards are well worth the effort for anyone interested in American history and awe-inspiring scenery.

Trip Description

Entry to the Harpers Ferry area depends on how early you arrive and the size of the tourist crowd. There is parking for about a dozen cars at the trailhead on Harpers Ferry Road, in Maryland, but these are almost always filled. Parking in Harpers Ferry proper, mostly around the old railroad station on Potomac Street, is very, very limited. Chances are good that you will have to park at the new contact station and Visitor Center on Cavalier Heights about a mile west of town. Information, wheelchair-accessible bathrooms, water, trash cans, and telephones are available there. An entry fee is charged. From this point, a shuttle bus will take you into Harpers Ferry.

The shuttle drops you on Shenandoah Street, where much of the restoration has taken place. Most of the buildings have the same appearance as they had during the Civil War; several may be entered and others have window displays. One contains bathrooms (which are not wheelchair accessible); another is a bookstore with offerings on the Civil War and Harpers Ferry. An information desk is staffed here as well. Most weekends find volunteer Civil War re-enactors wandering the lower town, and they give visitors a feel for what life was like here in the mid-nineteenth century.

The final block at the end of Shenandoah Street is Arsenal Square; small arms made in the US Musket factory nearby were stored in the arsenal building. John Brown's Fort, the old firehouse where Brown and his followers barricaded themselves after their ill-conceived raid on the arsenal, also stands here (although the original location was a short distance up Potomac Street on a site now occupied by the berm of the railroad).

At the intersection of Shenandoah and Potomac Streets is an open space adjacent to Arsenal Square. Known as the Point, it over-looks the confluence of the two rivers. A footbridge leads across the Potomac from here, and it is the start of this hike.

Opened in 1985, this bridge gives safe, legal access to the C&O Canal towpath and Maryland Heights on the far side of the river. It was originally exclusively a railroad bridge, but a pedestrian walk-way has now been built on one side, giving visitors an intimate view of the power and fury of a modern diesel as it roars by only yards away. On the way across, stop to look at the fine scenery. Below, the Potomac swirls deep and mysterious; upstream lie the rapids known as the Needles. Downriver, beautiful old stone bridge piers rise from the Potomac. These held the original railroad; the bridge was de-stroyed and rebuilt nine times during the Civil War. The flood of 1936 destroyed it for the final time, and the piers have stood alone in the river since then, a poignant reminder of the destructive pow-ers of both man and nature. Ahead, the nearly vertical shale cliffs of Maryland Heights are decorated with a huge advertisement now weathered into obscurity. Painted in 1895 or 1896, it says "Mennen's Borate Talcum Toilet Powder." Rock climbers occasionally rappel down the face.

The footbridge is also part of the historic Appalachian Trail (AT). Winding its way for more than 2,000 miles between Springer Moun-tain, Georgia, and Mount Katahdin, Maine, the AT is probably the world's most famous foot trail. Rerouted in 1985 with the completion of this footbridge, the AT now includes about a mile of travel in the town of Harpers Ferry. Harpers Ferry is the psychological if not the exact geographical halfway point, separating North from South. The town also houses the offices of the Appalachian Trail Conference, the primary source of maps, guidebooks, and other information for hikers.

At the Maryland end of the footbridge, a stairway leads down to the C&O Canal towpath. Turn left to follow the AT as it runs along the towpath. This section is quite beautiful, lined by tall sycamores and silver maples of great age and maturity. The Potomac runs fast through a series of rapids that extends downstream for about a mile. At high water, this stretch of river can be a killer, and even at summer low water the final rapids, White Horse, will flip most canoes. The interplay of water and rocks, however, makes a fascinating study from the safety of shore, and many hikers pause to relax with the sound of the river. On the opposite side of the towpath, spring rains often collect in the canal and provide breeding habitat for American toads and spring peepers. Orioles frequent the riverside trees in summer.

Continue for a quarter mile on the towpath to where a footbridge crosses the canal. Cross Harpers Ferry Road with care; the trailhead is immediately opposite. Two aspects of this trail are apparent: it is an old road, and it is steep. The road was built in 1861–62 by Union soldiers from Massachusetts to be used to access artillery positions atop Maryland Heights. Building a road over terrain as steep as this must have been a daunting task, especially since their only tools were pick and shovel, axe and saw, sweat and probably even some blood. Once the road was built, cannon were then hauled up it; one weighed almost 10,000 pounds and took more than 200 men to transport it. The statistics cannot be fully appreciated, however, until you hike up this quite literally breath-taking road, burdened only with water and some snacks.

At mile 0.7, bear right to visit the site of a naval battery that overlooks Harpers Ferry. There's a parapet with a deep trench behind it; the National Park Service rates the historic sites along this trail as among the best preserved of any in the United States from the Civil War era.

The trail now leads steeply uphill, rejoins the old military road, and soon comes to a fork. Stay right on the red-blazed Overlook Cliff Trail. At a second trail intersection about a quarter mile farther, stay right again. The trail now descends for almost a half mile to the cliffs overlooking Harpers Ferry.

This might not have been the view Thomas Jefferson wrote about, but it could have been, because the panorama laid out in front of you is truly dramatic. The two rivers, Shenandoah and Potomac, meld their waters several hundred feet directly below your perch, each river sparkling in the sun as it dances over rocks and rapids. The town of Harpers Ferry dozes at the nexus of the rivers, the old brick buildings lending an air of history to the place. Loudon

Heights in Virginia is the green mountain across the Potomac, one of a succession of hills visible marching into the hazy distance. Vultures soar overhead; pines release their perfumed resin scent on hot summer days; and hikers lounge about on the rocks taking in the remarkable view. Maryland Heights may be the best viewpoint in the Free State.

This view offers a good opportunity to look at the rock that forms both Maryland Heights and the Potomac riverbed. It is known generically as Harpers shale; the term encompasses the actual mudstone itself as well as several metamorphosed related forms.

About 600 million years ago, shallow seas covered this area. Sediments accumulated slowly over time in regular layers to a depth of from hundreds to thousands of feet. Over time, pressure compacted the mud into shale, and the decaying remains of shelled marine organisms into limestone.

This geological calm and its accompanying period of deposition changed relatively rapidly about 230 million years ago. Collision of crustal plates to the east exerted tremendous forces in a westward direction that resulted in a period of mountain building known as the Appalachian orogeny. The mountains, now called the Blue Ridge, rose to immense heights, rivaling the Rockies of today. Pressure and heat generated during this time metamorphosed many of the rocks, creating quartzite, schist, and slate.

Since that time, erosion has been at work, and the Blue Ridge is today only a shadow of its former self. The Potomac has cut through the bones of the Blue Ridge at Harpers Ferry, giving rise to the dramatic scenery of today. The layering effect so common to sedimentary rocks is seen in places along both this trail and the canal towpath, flat and level here, twisted and bent there. The more massive rock represents metamorphosed forms.

After enjoying the views, many hikers return to the trailhead by the same route, for a hike of 2.8 miles. However, history buffs, or those hikers in search of more challenges, will want to continue on the Stone Fort Trail. This trail begins at the intersection where the red-blazed Overlook Cliff Trail is at its highest point, 0.4 miles back from the overlook on the return trip. The Stone Fort trail has light blue blazes, and is clearly marked.

There is still a great deal of elevation to be attained on this trail; it goes steadily uphill, in places rather steeply, passing the locations of the 30 Pounder Battery and the 100 Pounder Battery, both marked with interpretive signs. After one mile on this trail, the apex is achieved at the Stone Fort. Built in 1862–63 by "contrabands" (ex-slaves freed by Union troops) to anchor the defenses atop Maryland Heights, the fort was never completed. However, there is still some fine stonework visible. The interior of the fort is grassy and it is a good place to rest and have a snack. The Stone Fort also marks the highest elevation on this trail, 1,448 feet above sea level, denoted by a brass survey disc.

From the Stone Fort, the trail leads downhill along a stone wall, the remains of breastworks erected here against attack from the north. An example of closing the barn door after the horse is already out, these defenses had not yet been contemplated when, in September 1862, Confederate forces marched southward down this ridge, forcing the undermanned garrison back into the town of Harpers Ferry after a brief firefight. Now controlling all three of the hills above the town, the Confederate Army under Thomas J. "Stonewall"

Jackson laid siege to the 14,000 Union soldiers in Harpers Ferry. It was a hopeless situation for the federal troops, who surrendered a few days later, on September 15. Had the Union garrison been able to hold out for another day or two, Jackson's men might not have arrived in Sharpsburg, Maryland, for the pivotal battle of Antietam on September 17, 1862.

Within a short distance southward from the wall, the trail joins the old road; follow it downhill for a mile to its intersection with the Overlook Cliff Trail. Bear right and continue to the trailhead after 5.2 miles. Return to Harpers Ferry, a one-way hike of 0.7 miles, to catch the shuttle bus up to Cavalier Heights and your car.

Directions

From the Baltimore Beltway (I-695), take I-70 west. From Washington, DC, take I-270 to I-70. In Frederick, exit onto Route 340 south. Cross the Potomac River, then the Shenandoah River, and continue to the well-marked park entrance (Cavalier Heights) at the top of the mountain.

Shorter routes through the countryside may be possible, especially for residents of northern Virginia.

Other Outdoor Recreational Opportunities Nearby

For the well-conditioned hiker, there are other trails in the area worth a visit. The Appalachian Trail rises out of the low point of Harpers Ferry by way of some steep climbs. In West Virginia, the trail is found a few feet from the south side of the Route 340 bridge over the Shenandoah River and leads up to Loudon Heights. In Maryland, the trail follows the canal towpath downriver for about two miles and then climbs steeply up Weverton Cliffs to the ridgetop of South Mountain. Fine views may be obtained from all these vantage points. A less aerobic choice would be the C&O Canal towpath, which extends westward from Harpers Ferry for 120 miles to Cumberland, Maryland, and eastward for 60 miles to Washington, DC.

PHYSIOGRAPHY OF MARYLAND

Travelers through Maryland often remark how diverse in appearance the state is. Indeed, Maryland has been described as "America in Miniature" because it has coast, flatlands, rolling hills, and mountains, all of which can be visited within an easy day's drive. The study of different landforms is called physiography, and Maryland has five different physiographic provinces. They are, proceeding from east to west, the Coastal Plain, the Piedmont, the Blue Ridge, the Ridge and Valley, and the Appalachian Plateau. A knowledge of the location of these zones, how they formed during the past history of the planet, and what each one looks like allows the scientist, naturalist, or interested visitor to make sense of the landscape and understand why certain plants and animals exist there.

Imagine getting into your car in Ocean City, Maryland, the easternmost point in the state, along the Atlantic coast, and driving west. The appearance of the land changes little for a long part of your drive, as you pass through the agricultural regions of the Eastern Shore, cross the Bay Bridge, and weave your way through the endless traffic of Anne Arundel County. The land is mostly flat, although it may have a few gentle hills, and if you took the time to get out of your car and feel the soil underfoot, most of it would be sandy. This is the Coastal Plain, where the rocks that form the earth's crust are buried far beneath layers of sand, gravel, silt, and other unconsolidated sediments.

Somewhere west of a line extending from Washington to Baltimore, you'll notice that the land becomes more rolling. Hills are higher, and rivers cut more deeply into the landscape. You are now in the Piedmont, named after an area in Italy with similarly rolling countryside. The transition from Coastal Plain to Piedmont appears gradual to the eye, but in fact it is a rather sharp demarcation if you examine either the soil or the flow of rivers and streams. Soils of the Piedmont are more complex. Sand plays a minimal role in such soils, and clays contribute much more. A spadeful of earth will be more difficult to obtain, since many small rocks will be present. Where rivers cut through the land, rock formations will be visible, and they create rapids where there is sufficient gradient. The final rapid on a river is called the fall line, and it often delineates the Piedmont from the Coastal Plain.

An hour's drive west through the Piedmont is a pleasant one, as the rolling hills get larger. Quite suddenly, just west of Frederick, a line of north-south–trending mountains appears, towering more than a thousand feet above the Piedmont. This is the Blue Ridge province, which in Maryland is actually composed of two roughly parallel ridges, Catoctin Mountain and South Mountain. In between lies the Middletown Valley. These are very old mountains in geological terms, having been worn down over the millennia to mere nubs of their former grand stature. Although they may look similar to the mountains farther to the west, they have a distinct origin and geology that make it worth our while to consider them as a unique physiographic province.

As you coast down the western side of the Blue Ridge, you soon enter the Ridge and Valley province. Here, too, are a series of north-south ridges, each pair separated by a small valley. However, the rock underlying the Ridge and Valley province is all sedimentary in nature, laid down in regular layers, and not at all like the massive blocks of metamorphic rock found in the Blue Ridge. The construction of I-68 through this region in the late 1980s and early 1990s tended to even out the dissected nature of the Ridge and Valley province for the automobile traveler; an alternate route on the Old National Pike (Scenic Route 40) gives a better flavor for the land.

Just west of Cumberland, you enter the final physiographic province of Maryland, the Appalachian Plateau. The road leads uphill for twelve miles, gaining 1,000 feet in elevation. This is the most dramatic change in physiography in Maryland; the plateau is significantly higher, colder, wetter, and less populated than the rest of the state.

Six hours driving time from Ocean City brings you to the West Virginia border. Behind you are roughly 300 miles of asphalt road, almost a half mile of elevation change, and five distinct physiographic provinces. Maryland may be called America in Miniature, but it has its own special flavor and character, which make it unique.

Catoctin Mountain Park

County: Frederick

Distance: 8.0 miles as described; circuit hike

Difficulty: Strenuous. Mountainous, with some quite steep sections; often rocky underfoot

Dogs: Permitted on leash

Why It's Special: A challenging hike in mountainous terrain with many rock outcroppings, a beautiful cascade, and several lovely views of the nearby valleys

More Information: Catoctin Mountain Park, www.nps.gov/cato, (301) 663-9388

Street Address: 6602 Foxville Road, Thurmont, Maryland 21788

GPS Coordinates: 39.634151, 77.449963 (Visitor Center)

Driving west from Maryland's population centers around Washington, DC, and Baltimore, one sees the Blue Ridge suddenly, hanging on the horizon like a dream. The escarpment rises abruptly from the rolling country of the Piedmont and marks the transition to western Maryland. With a geologic origin different from the rest of the state, the Blue Ridge is a unique physiographic province.

The Blue Ridge in Maryland is actually two parallel ridges, Catoctin Mountain to the east and South Mountain to the west, separated by the Middletown Valley. Only a dozen or so miles in width, the Blue Ridge is all that is left of a mountain range once as high as the present-day Alps. Over tens of millions of years, erosion has reduced these mountains to a few hard, erosion-resistant ridges of rock that we see protruding a thousand feet above the adjacent Piedmont. Where gaps in the forest cover exist, there are dramatic views eastward of the surrounding farmland and small towns.

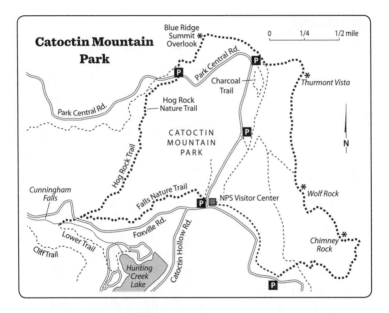

Most of Maryland's Blue Ridge is preserved in parkland. South Mountain, Greenbrier, Gambrills, and Cunningham Falls State Parks, the Frederick City watershed lands, the Appalachian Trail, and Catoctin Mountain Park all occupy the ridgetops and slopes of our narrowest physiographic province. All are scenic places to visit, but the best of the lot may be Catoctin. Here the mountains are higher, the buttressed ridges more deeply incised, and the streams more plentiful. Visitation is greatest in autumn, and for good reason; the display of fall color is exceptional, primarily due to the plentiful sugar maples, perhaps our prettiest autumn tree. Taken together, the geology, biota, and relatively short commute to the state's population centers make a hike in Catoctin Mountain Park a pleasant and enjoyable diversion.

This hike inscribes a loop almost entirely within the park boundaries and gives the hiker a feel for the Maryland Blue Ridge. While the total hiking distance is 8.0 miles as described, it's possible to bail out early if the trail proves too strenuous. I recommend starting at the park Visitor Center on Foxville Road (Route 77) and hiking in a clockwise direction so that the 700 feet of elevation change is spread over a longer distance.

Trip Description

Before you begin your hike, stop at the National Park Visitor Center at the intersection of Foxville Road (Maryland Route 77) and Park Central Road. The Depression-era stone building, built by the Civilian Conservation Corps, is lovely and has been modernized to provide necessary services without sacrificing its charm. There are bathrooms, drinking water, a small museum of local flora and fauna, and an information desk here. There is usually parking available in either the paved lot in front of the Visitor Center or in the unpaved lot across the road. Although the park map shows several alternative parking areas on the Park Central Road, be aware that this road is closed December through early April.

The first part of this trail, labeled the Falls Nature Trail on park maps, begins from the uphill end of the unpaved parking lot next to the Visitor Center. This wide and well-used trail is quite hilly, presaging the steep trail to come. It is also quite noisy, as it runs parallel to Route 77, although in warmer weather the leafy trees absorb some of that sound. While the trail passes through a forest, note that there are few really big trees. Most have a diameter of eighteen inches or less. Prior to 1935 when Catoctin was bought by the US government, this area was mostly marginal farmland and abandoned fields. Thus, even the largest trees are less than a century old.

The original tree cover began to be harvested in the late 1700s, when the nearby Monocacy valley was first settled. However, the most extensive timber cutting took place between 1859 and 1873, when the Catoctin Iron Furnace, just a few miles south, was in its heyday. More than 300 wood cutters were employed during this period. The wood was converted into charcoal on site, and then the charcoal was transported by wagon to the iron furnace. One thousand tons of pig iron required 160,000 bushels of charcoal, which in turn required 5,300 cords of wood. Before the end of the nineteenth century, then, this land looked very different than it does today; only along hard-to-reach steep-sided stream valleys were there any trees at all.

Even as the Catoctin forest grew and recovered, there were changes. American chestnut had been a dominant tree of the original forest, but by the time reforestation began in the 1930s, chestnuts were all but extinct, killed off by a fungal disease known as chestnut blight. Similarly, flowering dogwood was once a common understory tree, and the springtime forest was alive with its white flower petals.

But in the early 1980s, a fungal disease called anthracnose arrived in the Blue Ridge, killing more than 97 percent of Catoctin's dogwoods. The Catoctin forest we see today is much different from what the first settlers saw two hundred years ago.

After just over a mile, a well-marked trail junction is reached. This indicates a point where a short diversion from the Catoctin Loop is worthwhile. Turn left, carefully cross the busy Route 77, and step onto a boardwalk. This boardwalk carries you dryshod and safely across a wet, boulder-filled route leading to Cunningham Falls. This sloping cascade is Maryland's tallest waterfall (by a mere two feet as compared to Great Falls of the Potomac) as Big Hunting Creek flows over a large outcrop of metabasalt. Unfortunately, it is no longer possible to scramble over the rocks in search of the perfect photograph; you may only view the falls from the platform at boardwalk's end.

The forest around Cunningham Falls looks much different than it did just thirty years ago. Then, huge Eastern hemlock trees towered over the trails, casting a deep shade that kept this little valley cool on even the hottest days. Winters were especially beautiful, as white snow contrasted with the deep green needles of the hemlocks. In the 1990s, a tiny insect from Asia, the hemlock wooly adelgid, arrived and began to feed on hemlocks. Within a few years, many of the big trees near Cunningham Falls were dead. The park removed the hazardous snags and has now planted new hemlock seedlings protected from white-tailed deer browsing by wire cages. Every hemlock is now treated with an insecticide that kills the wooly adelgids. In another century, the area around Cunningham Falls will once again look like it did within recent memory.

Retrace your steps on the boardwalk, recross Route 77 with care, and begin a mile-long slog up a fairly steep trail toward Hog Rock. You'll climb almost 400 feet in elevation, but the scenery from Hog Rock is worth it; there are expansive views over the rolling countryside to the southeast. The overlook was named by local farmers who would bring their hogs to the base of the rock to fatten up on chestnuts and other mast that accumulated there. Hog Rock marks mile 2.6 of your 8-mile hike.

At this point, the trail joins the Hog Rock Nature Trail as it meanders across the top of the mountain. The forest here is dominated by sugar maple, a graceful and stately tree that rarely grows east of here. Unique among Maryland trees, sugar maples may turn crimson, orange, or yellow in autumn, a broad palette of natural color. In addition to their bright fall hues, sugar maples may be tapped each spring for their sweet sap, which is boiled to increase the sugar content of what then becomes maple syrup. The oldest trees date from the 1930s, when the land was last logged.

The trail soon crosses the Park Central Road, where there is a vault toilet (locked in winter), and then continues to the far side of the ridge. Here, the Blue Ridge Summit overlook gives distant views of the countryside between the arms of the Catoctins. Beyond this point, the trail continues in an up-and-down fashion for almost another mile to a trail junction. Bear left to continue this loop, but should you decide to cut short your hike, you can instead turn right and follow this trail downhill to the Visitor Center. Although the distance is more than a mile, the trail is all downhill and descends gradually.

If you have decided to pursue the hike as described, continue walking toward Thurmont Vista. The trail is well marked with a sign and proceeds eastward on a wide, gravel-paved treadway. While the first quarter mile is almost flat, the remaining 400 yards to the overlook are steep enough to get your attention. The reward is a beautiful view of the town of Thurmont and the well-ordered farmland that surrounds it. Thurmont Vista marks the halfway point of the Catoctin Loop Trail.

The trail now turns south to run along the eastern edge of the Blue Ridge, passing through a dry forest with an understory of lowbush blueberry and mountain laurel. Chestnut oak, the most common tree of ridgetops, dominates the canopy, although a mix of other oaks and sugar maples is present as well.

The next point of note is Wolf Rock, a 400-foot-long, 30-foot-high escarpment of quartzite that protrudes from the surrounding forest. A break in the rock cliff near the south end gives access, allowing a careful rock scramble over boulders and crevices. The quartzite forming most of Wolf Rock was originally sedimentary, sand grains that eroded off mountains to the west and accumulated in a shallow sea more than 500 million years ago. The collision of tectonic plates in the late Ordovician period caused these sediments to become compressed, heated, and folded into quartzite, an erosion-resistant rock. Quartzite outcroppings like Wolf Rock exist on the eastern edge of the Blue Ridge. Although the only view from Wolf Rock is over the treetops of the surrounding forest, it is still worth exploring. A few contorted pitch pines have managed to get a tenuous hold among these rocks, and their shade makes a pleasant site for lunch, a water break, or a snack. Pitch pine is easily identified: its needles are in groups of three, and the trunk is often "bearded" with needles.

A half-mile hike on a rocky trail brings you to Chimney Rock, another quartzite outcropping that has views southward over the hills of the Blue Ridge. Fall color is excellent in Catoctin Mountain Park, and this overlook is perhaps the best place to view it. Witch hazel, a small tree or large shrub, is common here. It is our latest-flowering plant species, and its yellow ribbon-like flower petals persist well into the winter and provide a bright splash of color to the otherwise drab late-autumn forest.

From Chimney Rock the trail drops more than 500 feet in one mile; it's wise to proceed slowly and with care as this downhill section is combined with a rocky footbed. The rock you are treading on is different from the quartzite seen at Wolf and Chimney Rocks. It is a gray-green rock called metabasalt that was originally a lava flow but was later metamorphosed by heat and pressure into its present form. This metabasalt is locally, colloquially, and aptly known as "greenstone."

When the trail reaches Foxville Road (Route 77), turn right at the sign indicating that the Visitor Center is one mile away. This portion of the trail runs parallel to the road, and even though it is about a hundred feet away and often above it, traffic noise mars the experience. In addition, the trail here is sometimes hard to follow, so pay close attention to its many twists and turns. After eight miles of excellent mountain hiking, arrive back at the Visitor Center.

Directions

From Washington, DC, take I-270 north and west to Frederick. From Baltimore, take I-70 west to Frederick. In Frederick, exit onto Route 15 north. Continue for about 15 miles on Route 15. Exit in Thurmont for Route 77. Proceed west on Route 77 for about three miles to the Catoctin Mountain Park Visitor Center.

Other Outdoor Recreational Opportunities Nearby

There is a wide variety of other hiking trails in Catoctin Mountain Park and the adjacent Cunningham Falls State Park; ask for details at the Visitor Center.

EASTERN HEMLOCKS AND HEMLOCK WOOLY ADELGIDS

The rising sun streams through the swirling morning mists, creating islands of light that dance across the forest floor and among the dark green needles of hemlock trees. The sound of birdsong drifts down from on high—Blackburnian and black-throated green warblers and the flutelike notes of wood thrushes echo among the trees. Large outcrops of mossy Catoctin greenstone litter the ground, giving the feel of a Bavarian landscape right out of some ancient fairy tale. In the 1980s, this trail to Cunningham Falls was as magical a place as existed anywhere in Maryland, visited by hundreds of people on most days, and perhaps thousands during prime fall color season.

But by 1990, something was wrong; the forest was sick. The stately old eastern hemlock trees that lent the characteristic deep shade here were diseased, their needles turning from dark green to gray and then falling to the earth. Naked branches appeared, and then storms felled some of the weakened trees. Sunlight reached the forest floor on a daily basis, and the red spiny canes of *Rubus* shrubs appeared. Jewelweed prospered in low, wet spots. The character of this Blue Ridge forest changed dramatically in the course of a decade.

The cause of all this ecological change was a tiny insect, often no larger than the period at the end of this sentence, called the hemlock wooly adelgid. This aphid-like sucking bug taps into the undersides of young stems where hemlock needles attach, siphoning off the sugary phloem that is the lifeblood of every tree. Visually, the presence of wooly adelgids is easily detected by white, waxy tufts secreted by the insect for protection from both predators and weather. Heavy infestations can directly kill a tree in four to ten years; more commonly, the trees are weakened, and succumb to disease or wind.

The eastern hemlock is an important tree species; one estimate indicates that it may host almost a thousand kinds of other organisms on its branches, needles, trunk, and roots. As such, it plays a significant role in forest ecology. A really large hemlock may be 150 feet tall, 6 feet in diameter, and live for more than 500 years, although most hemlocks in Maryland are much younger and smaller. They are highly shade tolerant, growing on steep slopes, especially along streams and rivers. Maryland has 42,000 acres of hemlock forests.

Unfortunately, there is no good way to treat large tracts of hemlock forests for wooly adelgids. Aerial spraying of broad-spectrum insecticides, as is done for gypsy moths, cannot be performed because most hemlocks grow along streams and creeks and the insecticide would kill nontarget aquatic insects as well. Instead, foresters are reduced to treating individual trees. When a tree is within fifty feet of water, the insecticide imidacloprid is injected into the trunk, where it spreads throughout the living tissue of the trees and into the phloem, which is siphoned off by the wooly adelgids. Between fall of 2014 and spring of 2015, exactly 6,497 hemlocks were treated by this laborious method. Farther from water, trees may be treated with the same chemical using soil drenches. In an experimental plot, such a treatment caused an 83 percent decline in wooly adelgids after one year, in contrast with a 34 percent decline (due to other factors) in the control plot. Another approach is biological control. There are several species of beetles that feed exclusively on wooly adelgids. *Laricobus nigrinus*, a predatory beetle native to the Pacific northwest, has been used for this purpose, but only 21,370 beetles were released between 2003 and 2015. While such biological control holds promise, the number of beetles produced by laboratory culture is still small, and their effectiveness is as yet uncertain.

The Department of Natural Resources has now begun to replant eastern hemlocks at Cunningham Falls State Park, taking special care of each young tree. It may take a century, but eventually future generations may yet enjoy the shady beauty of the hemlock forest there.

Green Ridge State Forest: Deep Run Trail

County: Allegany

Distance: 4.1 miles one way; out-and-back hike

Difficulty: Moderate. Surprisingly level but with a slight uphill trend; some creek crossings; some rocks and roots underfoot

Dogs: Permitted

Why It's Special: A pretty hike in a remote state-designated wildlands, with shale cliffs and rock outcrops

More Information: Green Ridge State Forest, http://dnr.maryland.gov /forests/Pages/publiclands/western_greenridgeforest.aspx, (301) 478-3124

Street Address: None available for trailhead

GPS Coordinates: 39.653029, 78.452289 (trailhead)

Green Ridge State Forest is one of Maryland's most familiar tracts of public land, while at the same time one of the least visited. It's familiar because anyone travelling to western Maryland must drive through Green Ridge; the Forest spans the length of the state, from the Pennsylvania border to the Potomac River. Interstate 68 in Allegany County passes through the mountainous heart of Green Ridge, revealing vistas of ridges and hollows, a landscape of trees uninterrupted by any sign of human habitation. At more than 47,000 acres, it is the largest block of public land in Maryland. And yet, it is lightly used, especially by hikers; it is primarily the realm of hunters and fishermen. There are no developed campgrounds, picnic areas, ballfields, playgrounds, or even available potable water. Roads are entirely unpaved, and although they are usually remarkably well maintained, they can be muddy and slippery in wet weather. What

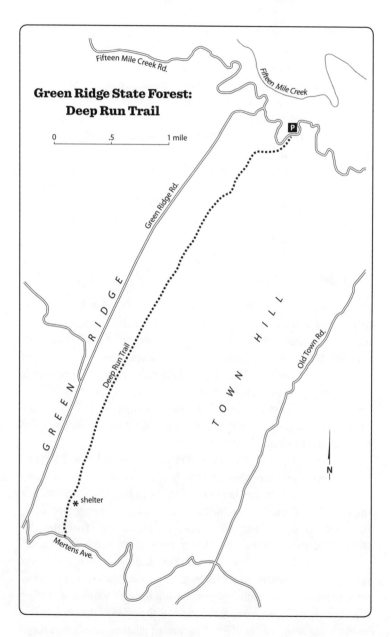

**Green Ridge State Forest:
Deep Run Trail**

Fifteen Mile Creek Rd.

Fifteen Mile Creek

0   .5   1 mile

Green Ridge Rd.

GREEN RIDGE

Deep Run Trail

TOWN HILL

Old Town Rd.

N

* shelter

Mertens Ave.

this means is that a hiker at Green Ridge experiences a surprising degree of solitude, even a wilderness character, that is rarely encountered in most state parks.

There are twenty-four miles of designated hiking trails in Green Ridge. The best may be the Deep Run Trail, 4.1 miles in length, and it is described here. The Deep Run Trail passes through a State Wildland, an area set aside for its ecological, geological, scenic, and contemplative values. (Such areas typically contain plant or animal species of special concern, or may have wilderness characteristics. Only passive recreation is allowed in Wildlands, like hiking, birding, hunting, and fishing. Importantly, logging is banned, which permits the ecology of the area to mature without management.) Set in a deep valley in the heart of Green Ridge, the Deep Run Trail gets little use but is well maintained. Perhaps surprisingly in this land of steep ridges, the trail runs almost flat, with only about 300 feet of elevation change in four miles.

Trip Description

Begin your hike from the northernmost trailhead, where Fifteen Mile Creek Road crosses Deep Run. There is limited parking here, for perhaps four or five vehicles in dry weather, but only one when roadside pullouts are muddy. Sign in at the trailhead register before proceeding up the trail. Even if you don't have a map, it's impossible to get lost; the trail occupies a very narrow floodplain with hills on both sides for its entire length to Mertens Avenue. The Deep Run Trail is well marked with green diamonds on a white field; you will never be out of sight of one of these blazes.

The first mile of the Deep Run Trail is arguably the prettiest and most interesting (in ecological terms). Shale cliffs and steep slopes with shale outcroppings border the creek to the left. Laid down in the Devonian Period about 380 million years ago, these sedimentary rocks were once mud flats, alluvial soils washed down from the Blue Ridge Mountains to the east. When the African and North American tectonic plates collided about 300 million years ago, a series of north/south trending ridges formed, like wrinkles in a rug that you push from one edge. Subsequent erosion created valleys, like Deep Run, between ridges like those rising to either side of the trail. In this fashion, the deeply dissected landscape of what is now Green Ridge State Forest formed.

Shale slopes are often dry, with poorly developed soil where there is any at all. Three factors contribute to these xeric conditions. First,

this area receives the least rainfall of any part of Maryland. While an average year sees about 40 inches of rain across most of the state, 25–30 inches is typical here. Second, shale is fissured by tiny cracks that drain rainfall below the root zone of any plants. Finally, soils derived from shale tend to have tiny flakes of that parent rock, and so on steep slopes those soils erode easily.

The shale cliffs on the east side of the Deep Run Trail create a deep shade over the waters of the creek. Deep Run is neither very deep nor wide; in summer and fall, the flow is only a trickle, and the dozen or so crossings are easy rock-hops. In spring, however, you may get your feet wet at these places. A glance at the topographic map of this area reveals an interesting observation: no streams at all drain the west side of Deep Run, while fully a dozen streams feed into the east side. Thus, the southeast-facing hillsides are dry, with few understory plants, whereas the northwest-facing slopes have more vegetation. In the narrow valley itself, where there are actual humus-containing soils and more moisture, there are good displays of spring wildflowers and abundant ferns, including Christmas, interrupted, and hay-scented ferns. The trail itself is so lightly used that mosses, grasses, and even a few wildflowers carpet the treadway.

After the first half mile, the shale cliffs give way to slopes with only the occasional rocky outcrop. Sugar maples are common, and in the second half of the trail the forest becomes more diverse, with white pines, oaks, tulip poplars, and hickories dominating the overstory and spicebush and witch hazels the understory. Since Deep Run is in the center of a huge block of contiguous forest, there are commendably few non-native plants.

The trail continues with only a slight uphill rise to it. Rock and roots litter the path, but they are rarely large enough to stumble over. There are several mileage markers (although some are missing). Each is a yellow metal pole with two numbers; the upper number is the number of miles you have walked from the trailhead behind you, while the lower number refers to how many miles you still have to walk to reach the upcoming trailhead. After almost four miles, there is a three-sided log shelter available for overnight use by backpackers. Another quarter mile brings you to the Mertens Avenue trailhead, 4.1 miles from Fifteen Mile Creek Road. If you have only a single car, you have reached the halfway point of your hike; return by the same route.

Should you have a second car with your group, available for a shuttle, you have two options. Park it at Mertens Avenue for the described four-mile hike, or park it at Kirk Avenue and walk another three miles south on what eventually is named the Big Run Trail. The Deep Run Trail ultimately reaches a height of land between the ridges, marking the point at which you enter the south-flowing watershed of Big Run. One advantage of this longer hike is that by walking a short distance west on Kirk Road, you reach the Log Roll Overlook, with stunning views of the Town Creek valley almost a thousand feet below.

Directions

From Baltimore or Washington, take I-70 west. At Hancock, branch onto I-68 west. Continue for 18 miles, then take exit 62 south onto Fifteen Mile Creek Road. After this road turns to gravel, continue for about a mile to the trailhead, where there is a signpost.

Other Outdoor Recreational Opportunities Nearby

There are other hiking trails at Green Ridge; ask for information at headquarters. The southern border of the Forest is the Potomac River, where there is hiking and cycling on the C&O Canal towpath and paddling on a section of the Potomac called the Paw Paw Bends.

FOREST FRAGMENTATION

When Maryland was first colonized, almost all of the state was covered by mature forests. Chestnuts, oaks, hickories, and other species typical of Appalachian old-growth forests shaded rich, complex soils that harbored an abundance of wildflowers. Streams and rivers dissecting the forest flowed clear and clean, even after heavy rains. Animal life was abundant, although it tended toward insects, salamanders, and songbirds rather than species we tend to think of as "game." This primeval forest had evolved over thousands of years into a stable, diverse ecosystem, the likes of which we will never see again.

Today, only about 41 percent of Maryland is covered with forests, and most of that is in early or mid-successionary stages that in terms of structure, diversity, energy flow, and function bear only slight resemblance to a mature old-growth forest. Furthermore, most of the forests that do remain exist as patches distributed irregularly about the landscape, separated from each other like islands in the sea. In this sense, the forest has been fragmented, and this fragmentation has major implications for the plants and animals that live there.

Scientists have long known that fragmentation reduces the diversity of organisms and renders populations more susceptible to extinctions. The number of species that a tract can hold relates to its size, but this species-area relationship is not linear or simple. The best example of this correlation is found among certain species of migratory songbirds. Many of our neotropical migrants nest in the interior of forests and thus require a rather large parcel of undisturbed, mature forest. Examples include ovenbirds,

(continued)

worm-eating warblers, veeries, and acadian flycatchers. In one study, red-eyed vireos were found in virtually 100 percent of woodlots between 50 and 75 acres in size but in only 10 percent of woodlots between 17 and 42 acres.

The degree of disturbance needed for "fragmentation" depends on the species affected; in some cases, even strip development, such as that for highways, power line cuts, or dirt logging roads, is sufficient to affect some animals. For example, it has been shown that female cowbirds use narrow strip corridors like dirt roads to provide access to the inside of large tracts of forest, where they parasitize the nests of forest interior–dwelling birds. Similarly, even small clearcuts where trees are logged from the interior of a large forest may have dramatic effects on relatively sessile species like salamanders. Salamanders rarely move more than a few hundred yards (and sometimes less) in their lifetimes. It is not unusual for a researcher who marks a woodland salamander to come back the next year and find it under the same rock. Most scientists believe that when salamander habitats are disturbed, many animals die rather than migrate.

Data such as these have prompted scientists and knowledgeable conservationists to call for the maintenance of our forests in large, unbroken tracts. In Maryland, such larger woodlands are mostly in public hands, on our state forests. Unfortunately, more than 50 percent of the acreage on these forests is managed for timber harvesting, and the most common harvest method, clearcutting, is carried out in a patchwork of small plots. Clearly, this process greatly fragments the forest, diluting the value of the forest acreage that remains. If logging has to occur on Maryland state forests (and many citizens feel that it need not), management decisions should be driven by consideration for the full spectrum of wildlife and multiple use values rather than merely harvesting trees for their economic value. Longer rotations between harvests, a ban on clearcutting, and wider use of peripheral cuts are all timber management techniques that reduce fragmentation and can be instituted on our state forests without significantly affecting the viability of the logging industry.

Monroe Run Trail

County: Garrett

Distance: 4.6 miles one way; out-and-back hike

Difficulty: Moderate. Relatively flat, surprisingly few rocks underfoot, but many stream crossings

Dogs: Permitted

Why It's Special: A beautiful, moderately easy hike in a forested vale rich in wildflowers and shaded by mature trees

More Information: Savage River State Forest, http://dnr.maryland.gov /forests/Pages/savageguide.aspx, (301) 895-5759; Big Run State Park, http://dnr.maryland.gov/publiclands/Pages/western/bigrun.aspx, (301) 895-5453

Street Address: 10368 Savage River Road, Swanton, Maryland 21561 (trailhead)

GPS Coordinates: 39.549318, 79.145976 (trailhead)

Ahhh. . . . Western Maryland! Great place for a vacation: cooler summer temperatures, beautiful fall color, activities around Deep Creek Lake—it just doesn't get any better. But hiking? Don't think so—all those mountains. Huffing and puffing up steep hills, climbing over and around boulders, stumbling over rocks in the treadway—doesn't sound like fun.

If that's you, here is a hiking trail you're bound to like. Following an old road constructed by the Civilian Conservation Corps in the 1930s, the Monroe Run Trail proceeds almost dead flat for four miles. Rarely do you have to look down to make sure you won't trip over rocks or tree roots in this well-maintained path. The scenery is drop-dead gorgeous, with big trees that turn every shade of red, orange, and yellow in autumn, as diverse an assemblage of spring wildflowers as you'll find anywhere in the Free State, and summer days that are shady and naturally cool.

All set to hike? Well, there is one little thing you need to know. The trail crosses Monroe Run. Not just once. Not just a few times. But seventeen distinct crossings, every one of which will require you to get your feet wet in all but the longest season of drought. And if you do this hike as an out-and-back walk, to avoid the long car shuttle between trailheads, that number doubles to thirty-four. I know—I counted them. The key to an enjoyable day is to plan in advance for these fluvial adventures. I recommend wearing hiking sandals or river sandals that you've broken in thoroughly and are used to wearing and walking in. If you do so, the Monroe Run Trail will be an eminently enjoyable and unforgettable hike.

The Monroe Run Trail is maintained and managed by the Savage River State Forest, although the primary trailhead is in Big Run State Park. Red blazes mark the trail, but they are hardly needed; the path is always clearly evident, and the terrain prevents any side trails branching off toward an unknown destination. The total length of the trail is 4.6 miles. Only the final half mile has any significant elevation change to it, but this portion does climb steeply to the other trailhead on New Germany Road. I recommend this hike as an out-and-back excursion, but suit yourself.

Trip Description

Begin your hike from the downstream trailhead in Big Run State Park. The campsites at Big Run are primitive (pit toilets, no water) but beautiful, shaded by large trees; they cannot be reserved in advance. Big Run is located on the banks of the Savage River Reservoir, nestled in the heart of the mountains. It's off the beaten path, but well worth the trip.

The Monroe Run Trail begins adjacent to campsite 68, entering a vale bordered by steep hills but with a flat floodplain perhaps seventy yards wide. The forest here is a mix of eastern hemlocks and hardwoods like oaks, hickories, and maples, all mature trees that cast a deep shade on the forest floor. In summer the nearby stream generates humidity that is held in place by these trees, creating early-morning mists that swirl in the chilly air.

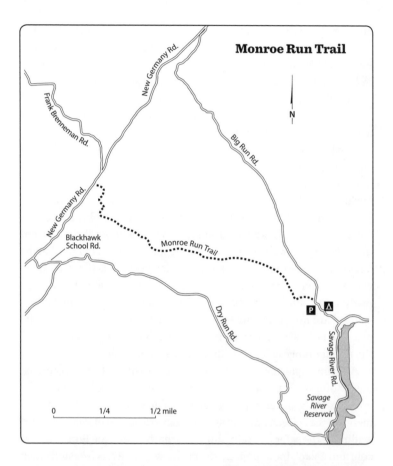

The many hemlocks along Monroe Run seem to be holding their own against the attacks of wooly adelgids. These tiny insects, the size of period at the end of this sentence, first arrived in the United States from Asia accidentally in 1951 and have since spread throughout much of the eastern hemlock's range. The insects suck the sap from hemlock needles, eventually killing the tree outright or weakening it to the extent that death from other causes may occur. The presence of the wooly adelgid is most easily noted when wooly white egg cases appear on branches.

Considerable success has been achieved in fighting the wooly adelgid, but the several kinds of treatments are expensive and diffi-cult to apply to large stands of hemlocks in remote areas. The most environmentally friendly method is to apply a horticultural oil as a sprayed drench on individual trees. A chemical insecticide, imidacloprid, is quite effective, but must be injected into trees on an individual basis. Some success with biological control has also been achieved, using one of several species of beetle that feed specifically on wooly adelgids. Both imidacloprid and beetles are currently being used in the Monroe Run area.

Eastern hemlock is the dominant tree in this forest, and the species is home to several kinds of songbirds who nest and feed here in late spring and early summer. Among the most beautiful of these birds are Blackburnian warblers and black-throated green warblers, both of whom are specifically associated with hemlocks. These tiny, active birds that hang out in the treetops are difficult to spot, but their lively, distinctive, and complex songs are often heard filtering down from the canopy. One especially vigorous black-throated green was observed to sing 466 times in an hour. And Blackburnians typically sing a different song at midday than at dawn and dusk. Both species are attractive birds, but the Blackburnian holds a special place in the hearts of birders; it is fondly known as "the firethroat" for the bright orange coloration in the upper thorax region.

Within a quarter mile, the trail reaches the first of many crossings of Monroe Run. Although you may be able to rock-hop across the creek in dry weather, slippery and unstable stones underfoot (not to mention the sixteen remaining crossings still ahead of you) argue for wading as the safer and refreshing alternative. Monroe Run is always cold and clear, since virtually the entire watershed is forested. Such pristine conditions often permit native brook trout to live and prosper. However, the first four miles of Monroe Run have little change in elevation, and so lack the rapids and small waterfalls that provide ideal trout habitat. Although Monroe Run does harbor brook trout, the nearby Savage River and its tributary creeks, renowned for their superb fishing opportunities, may be a better choice for anglers. (Most of the creeks in the Savage River State Forest are catch-and-release, zero creel limit streams; be sure to check regulations.)

A diverse assemblage of spring wildflowers enlivens the floodplain and adjacent slopes along Monroe Run. Indeed, this trail is a garden of botanical delights. Among the common species are wild geranium, May apple, dwarf ginseng, red trillium, foamflower, jack-in-the-pulpit, wild ginger, sweet white violet, trout lily, and extensive stands of blue cohosh. Unfortunately, another member of the vegetable kingdom grows trailside in profusion: stinging nettles. The syringe-like trichomes lining the stem of this perennial herb deliver a burning, itching sting to the exposed skin of any hiker who ambles by, innocently unaware. For twenty minutes or so, the torture is exquisite until the skin's defenses finally break down the chemicals (acetylcholine, serotonin, and histamine) that cause this inflammatory response. If stung, treat with hydrocortisone cream, or, in a pinch, mud.

The trail continues up-valley in a direct fashion as Monroe Run meanders from one side to the other. At many of the stream crossings, the remains of reinforcing stonework can be seen, laid down for the roadbed by the Civilian Conservation Corps workers in the 1930s. It excites the imagination to contemplate what working in this remote valley must have been like for young men in the Depression, so far from home and family. The sheer quantity of CCC construction in parks and forests around the state is astounding, and much of it is still extant.

The width of the Monroe Run valley gradually narrows, and shade-loving hemlocks and rhododendrons become even more common. Here, where springs and seeps supply water to Monroe Run, is perfect habitat for salamanders. These sensitive amphibians breathe through their skin and so are acutely affected by pollution, water temperature, and the amount of acidity in the water. Eastern red-backed, valley and ridge, and slimy salamanders can sometimes be found under woody debris in wet areas.

Finally, after almost four miles of relatively flat trail, the pathway leaves Monroe Run behind, climbing uphill at a fairly steep but steady rate. Its historic nature as a road becomes evident, as the trail is now wide enough for a vehicle. Within a half mile or so, the path reaches New Germany Road, where there is off-road parking at the trailhead. There is nothing special about this portion of the Monroe Run Trail; most hikers turn around when the trail starts uphill, walking in the reverse direction back to their car at Big Run State Park.

Directions

From Washington, DC, or Baltimore, take I-70 west. Near Hancock exit onto I-68 west. Take exit 22, Chestnut Ridge Road, south for

2 miles. Go left onto New Germany Road. Go 5 miles. Make a left onto Big Run Road. Go almost 5 miles; look for the Big Run State Park campsites and park. The trail begins behind site 68.

Other Outdoor Recreational Opportunities Nearby

There are many hiking trails within a thirty-minute drive of the Monroe Run trailhead. New Germany State Park is nearby and has a complex of trails that are especially popular in winter for cross country skiing. Maryland's best fly fishing for brook trout may be found on the Savage River upstream of the reservoir and Big Run State Park.

THE DECLINE OF FOREST SONGBIRDS II: CAUSES

That forest songbirds, especially those that migrate each autumn to the neotropics, have been declining is now undisputed. The causes of this thorny problem in conservation biology, however, are still hotly debated by amateur birders and professional ornithologists alike. Until all the contributing factors are better understood, it could be that we will be powerless to improve the situation. What are some of the best hunches scientists have about the decline of eastern forest songbirds?

One of the difficulties in sorting out this problem is that neotropical migrants live in not one but three habitats separated in space and time: their breeding grounds, their wintering grounds, and their migration route. These birds spend about half the year in the tropics, scattered throughout Mexico, Central and South America, and the Caribbean. Development there, especially conversion of large tracts of tropical old-growth forests to slash-and-burn agriculture, may contribute to the problem. However, recent investigations have shown that many species of neotropical migrants can use a variety of agricultural, scrub, and second-growth habitats on the wintering grounds. For this reason, researchers now believe that, with the exception of certain species with narrow winter habitat requirements, factors associated with the summer breeding grounds in North America constitute the most significant threats to neotropical bird populations.

Loss of habitat here at home is undoubtedly a major culprit. Everyone knows a favorite woods or birding spot that has fallen to development. That means that wildlife residents of that plot of land have to move on and find other suitable habitat or they will perish. Birds, at least, are mobile and can search a large area rather quickly for new habitat, but such islands of suitable habitat become smaller and more distant from each other every year.

Related to habitat loss is fragmentation: the constant encroachment of development on remaining tracts of forest, splitting them into ever smaller chunks. Most species of forest songbirds are "area-sensitive"; fledging of young is far more successful in large tracts of unbroken, mature forest than in smaller parcels split by roads or power lines and surrounded by a sea of agricultural lands. This is because small tracts have a higher ratio of "edge" to "interior" relative to large tracts. Such "edge" habitat, as well as artificial corridors leading to the interior of an otherwise unfragmented parcel of forest, provides access for predators like raccoons, jays, crows, foxes, and domestic animals. To examine the effect of such predators on bird eggs and nestlings, scientists placed artificial nests stocked with quail eggs in forests of varying sizes. Small suburban woodlots showed almost 100 percent predation of nests, whereas the largest forest tracts had almost none. In addition to predation, brood parasitism by brown-headed cowbirds is also a major problem, especially in smaller woodlands.

Finally, neotropical migrants may be affected by at least two threats that are only now beginning to be appreciated. When the gypsy moth arrived in Maryland in the 1980s, the state responded aggressively with spraying campaigns in many Maryland forests. The two most common insecticides, Dimilin and Bacillus thuringiensis, affect the caterpillar stage of woodland insects, which form the primary food of many forest songbirds. Butterflies and moths become less common after forests are treated with insecticidal sprays; no doubt other insects, less obvious to us humans but important food for birds, are equally negatively

(continued)

affected. Still another potential threat to those birds that nest on the ground and in low vegetation may be the state's burgeoning populations of white-tailed deer. In areas with lots of deer, vegetative cover can be eaten to the ground, exposing nests to higher levels of predation. Studies in which deer are excluded by fencing in Shenandoah National Park have shown how vegetative defoliation affects the nesting success of birds.

What can be done to save our avian natural heritage? First, preservation of critical wintering habitat in its natural state will be important. Scientists have only recently identified such habitats, and work continues on this project in the tropics. Second, critical stopover areas during migration must also be preserved. The value of such stopover points has been well established for migrating shorebirds, but the locations of similar stopovers for songbirds have not been carefully cataloged, primarily because they are more disperse in time and space. Finally, in Maryland and surrounding mid-Atlantic states, we should preserve our public forests in large unbroken tracts. In order to do so, these forests must begin to be managed for the full diversity of plants and animals present rather than merely for game animals and lumber production.

If there is any good news about neotropical migrant songbirds, it is that the marked downward trend in numbers noted between 1966 and about 2000 has leveled off in the last decade, at least for some species. Ovenbirds, American redstarts, blue-gray gnatcatchers, and hooded, yellow, and parula warblers are all holding steady of late in Maryland. These successes may be due in part to preservation of large blocks of forest without fragmentation, as the understanding of forest disturbance's deleterious effects on forest interior dwelling bird species has become more widely understood. However, very few of these species are actually increasing in numbers; what we see is that a revised baseline, a "new normal," has been established against which future gains or losses will be measured. As the years go by, fewer birders and scientists are around to recall the halcyon days of the early to mid-twentieth century, and that memory is lost forever.

Lostland Run Trail

County: Garrett

Distance: 3.5 miles one way; out-and-back hike

Difficulty: Moderate. Rocky treadway underfoot, several stream crossings, a few short, steep hills

Dogs: Permitted

Why It's Special: A lightly used, beautiful trail along a tumbling mountain stream shaded by big trees with lots of rhododendrons and wildflowers

More Information: Potomac State Forest, http://dnr.maryland.gov/wildlife /Pages/NaturalAreas/Western/Lostland-Run.aspx, (301) 334-2038; Garrett Trails, http://garretttrails.org/, (301) 387-3013

Street Address: 1431 Potomac Camp Road, Oakland, Maryland 21550 (Potomac State Forest Headquarters and trailhead)

GPS Coordinates: 39.378733, 79.282915 (trailhead)

The Lostland Run Trail is one of two described in this book that drop off the Appalachian Plateau to the Potomac River below (the second is the Monroe Run Trail). Although they share a common physiography, and are only a dozen or so miles apart, they are quite distinct in appearance and in the suite of wildflowers for which they are so justly admired. Taken together, these two trails constitute a perfect duo for a weekend of hiking in western Maryland.

The Lostland Run Trail is an out-and-back hike of seven miles, but that distance can be halved by the use of two cars for a shuttle. A gravel and stone road runs parallel to and never more than 100 yards from the trail (useful in case of emergency), and there is a large parking area at the far end near the Potomac River. Along the Lostland Run Trail, there are two very different scenic viewpoints that are among the best in Maryland—Cascade Falls and Potomac Overlook. Fall color is superb. The trail is lightly used (wildflowers grow in the middle of the foot path in some places), not at all well constructed, and irregularly maintained. There are six places where the trail crosses Lostland Run and you will need to wade in the creek, at least in spring or after substantial rain. Still, there are few hikes in Maryland as beautiful as the Lostland Run Trail.

Trip Description

Begin your hike from the headquarters of the Potomac/Garrett State Forest in the southern part of Garrett County, well away from the hubbub of Deep Creek Lake and its vacation crowds. There are maps and information available here, as well as water and restrooms. The Lostland Run Trail begins just across the road at a signboard and trail register. White blazes mark the route.

Initially, the trail passes through a forest whose soil is a gnome's fairyland of rocks and boulders, ranging in size from that of a basketball to that of a small automobile. All are covered in mosses and lichens, yellow-green in drought and bright green when wet. The trail winds among and over these boulders, sometimes muddy underfoot, sometimes rocky, but always requiring careful foot placement. The forest is a mixture of hardwoods and hemlocks; few are exceptionally large in this commercially logged forest, but many are approaching maturity. After a half mile of this pleasant but unexceptional scenery, the trail reaches Lostland Run at a point where a two-story cylindrical tank sits above the creek.

This structure is a lime doser. There are many abandoned coal mines in Garrett County that leak acid-tainted water into local streams, killing fish and virtually all other forms of aquatic life. One way to correct this acidic water pollution is to add lime (calcium carbonate), which helps to neutralize the acidity of the water. This lime doser adds small amounts of calcium carbonate to Lostland Run on a regular basis, and native brook trout again live in this beautiful mountain stream.

The entire length of the Lostland Run Trail is exceptionally rich in spring wildflowers. Blooming in early- to mid-May, perhaps the most showy are three species of trillium: red, white, and painted. As the name implies, the floral structures come in groups of three, symmetrically arranged: three leaves, three sepals, three petals, a tripartite pistil, and six stamens. Trilliums are long-lived plants, requiring

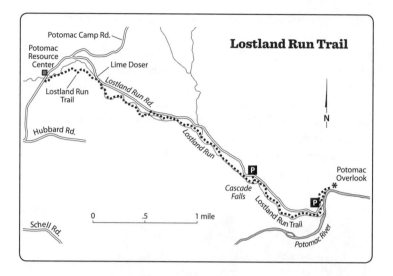

as much as seven years of vegetative growth before flowering. Other spring flowers common here (but not on the nearby Monroe Run Trail) include bluebead lily and perfoliate bellwort.

In the mile downstream of the lime doser, the trail crosses Lostland Run six times. You may be able to find steppingstone rocks that permit dryshod crossing at lower water levels, but there are no guarantees. The trail along this section of creek was recently rerouted, due to landslides and impassable tangles of fallen trees, so the map provided by the Maryland Department of Natural Resources may not be correct. White blazes are frequent on the Lostland Run Trail, so keep alert to their presence as you find your route.

Soon after the sixth and final crossing of the creek, the trail arrives within view of a three-sided building (Red Pine shelter) that may be reserved for overnight use. The surrounding area has plenty of flat space for tents, but the campsite is sometimes trash-strewn. Within sight of the shelter, the trail crosses the North Prong on a rickety, swaying suspension bridge.

The next half mile of trail is lightly used, with occasional downed trees and erosion, but the path is always obvious. The steep, rocky slopes along Lostland Run are home to the long-tailed shrew, a mouse-sized mammal that feeds voraciously on insects, spiders, and other invertebrates. Found only at higher elevations in the Appalachian Mountains, long-tailed shrews require rock-strewn terrain with many crevices where they both hunt for prey and shelter from larger predators.

Occupying the same habitat along Lostland Run is the southern rock vole, a chubby, short-tailed rodent that feeds primarily on vegetation, especially the fruits of native wildflowers. This vole creates burrows and runways under and around piles of rock and woody debris, especially in damp areas with lots of moss and ferns. Despite being an animal of the Appalachian Mountains, where the winters are long and severe, rock voles do not hibernate, remaining active throughout the year.

At mile 2.7, a set of wooden steps leads down to a scenic highlight of the Lostland Run Trail, Cascade Falls. Here the creek drops about twenty feet over a series of stairstep ledges set in a hemlock-shaded dell. This idyllic scene invites the hiker to pause, relax, and perhaps bathe trail-weary feet in the icy water. Cascade Falls is a very photogenic place.

To continue hiking downstream on the Lostland Run Trail, ascend the wooden staircase and look to the right for white slashes painted on trees. For the next hundred yards or so, the trail traverses slabs of loose rock that may shift alarmingly underfoot and that obscure the direction taken by the trail. Keep alert and follow the blazes, however, and eventually the trail will widen and become more obvious. Within another half mile, there is a sturdy footbridge over Lostland Run that provides views downstream to where the creek enters the North Branch of the Potomac River. Don't cross the footbridge, however, but instead follow what is now a dirt road about 100 yards to the gravel parking lot at the end of Lostland Run Road.

Be sure to take the footpath, located at the downstream end of the parking lot, to Potomac Overlook. Within 100 yards, this trail leads to a beautiful view of the North Branch where that river curves ninety degrees westward. Photographs of this vista, with the river tumbling over rocks and rapids in a wild gorge, are often featured in literature promoting the scenic beauty of Garrett County.

If you have set up a car shuttle for this hike, your vehicle awaits you either in the parking lot or a few dozen yards up the road. (The last short segment of Lostland Run Road is steep and rocky, suitable only for high clearance vehicles.) Otherwise, retrace your steps on the Lostland Run Trail upstream for 3.5 miles to the parking lot at the trail's origin on Potomac Camp Road at the ranger station.

Directions

From Washington, DC, or Baltimore take I-70 and I-68 west. Beyond Frostburg, take exit 19, Route 495, south for 25 miles. Turn left on Boiling Spring Road, pass through the tiny town of Deer Park, and continue for about 2.5 miles. Turn right on Eagle Rock Road. Go 0.9 miles. Turn left on Bethlehem Road. Go 1.4 miles. Turn left on Combination Road. Go 0.6 miles. Turn left on Potomac Camp Road and follow it to the Potomac State Forest headquarters parking lot and trailhead on the left.

Other Outdoor Recreational Opportunities Nearby

There are several other hiking trails on the Potomac State Forest; since the trailhead is the forest headquarters, ask there for information. Swallow Falls State Park is about a thirty-minute drive away. The Monroe Run Trail is also about a thirty-minute drive away.

ACIDIC DEPOSITION IN MARYLAND

Few people are aware that Maryland has some of the most acidic rainfall in the United States. The average pH of rain in Maryland is about 4.3, approximately twelve times more acidic than the typical pH of 5.6 for unpolluted rain. In addition to acid rain, acidic solids from power plants and automobile exhausts also fall on Maryland, and all three together are referred to as acidic deposition. This process has some important effects on aquatic organisms across the state.

The source of much of this acidic deposition lies outside Maryland. More than 50 percent of acidic deposition in the mid-Atlantic states comes from just fifty coal-burning power plants located to our west and concentrated along the Ohio River. Nevertheless, we residents are not without blame; the failure of Baltimore and Washington to meet federal air quality standards is primarily due to the level of pollution from automobile exhaust.

In some areas of Europe, acidic deposition has affected the trees growing in remote forests. Maryland's forests have not yet been significantly affected as far as we know; most of the damage has been to aquatic ecosystems, especially small streams. About one-third of all headwater streams in Maryland, more than 2,600 miles of such streams, are either sensitive to potential acidification or already acidic. Most of these creeks are located on the Appalachian Plateau in Garrett County or on the Coastal Plain surrounding Chesapeake Bay.

What makes a stream susceptible to damage by acidic deposition? In addition to the pH of rainfall and the amount of dry acids deposited, the single most important factor is the buffering capacity of the soils through which the water flows. The limestone-containing soils of the Ridge and Valley province, for example, have almost unlimited buffering capacity and can neutralize precipitation of any acidity.

Stream organisms exhibit differing levels of sensitivity. Mussels and some aquatic insect larvae like stonefly larvae need water of pH 6 or better. Brown trout and some salamanders die off at pHs less than 5. Scavenging beetles like water boatmen and whirligig beetles can persist down to pH 3.5, although they may be indirectly affected by damage to the food chain. In western Maryland streams, the presence of a diverse fish community is correlated with water pH and buffering capacity.

In Coastal Plain streams, ephemeral pulses of acidic water, rather than a continuous low pH, have had biological effects. During the winter, acid deposition can become trapped in snow. When the snow melts suddenly, the solubilized acidity is released as a sudden pulse. If this occurs late in the winter, the acid spike may reach the spawning grounds of anadromous fish like shad, rockfish, blueback herring, and white perch. Embryos of these fish have been shown to be killed by such pulses of acidity, and the decline of these species is due at least in part to such acid effects.

Kendall Trail

County: Garrett

Distance: Up to 5.7 miles one way; out-and-back hike

Difficulty: Easy. Mostly flat but often rocky underfoot; muddy in spring and wet weather

Dogs: Permitted on leash

Why It's Special: A relatively easy hike into a remote and beautiful wild river canyon, Maryland's only designated Wild and Scenic River

More Information: Town of Friendsville, http://friendsville.org/kendall-trail/; Garrett Trails, http://garretttrails.org/, (301) 387-3013

Street Address: 701 Morris Avenue, Friendsville, Maryland 21531 (trailhead)

GPS Coordinates: 39.661978, 79.407378 (trailhead)

The Youghiogheny River in the far northwestern corner of the state is one of Maryland's most remote and beautiful places; in fact, it is our only officially designated Scenic River that also meets the stringent requirements for "Wild" classification. With much of the river bank land privately held, the ten-mile canyon from Sang Run to Friendsville was for decades almost completely inaccessible to the public. But in 1974, local kayakers discovered that the "Upper Yough" (pronounced "Yock"), as this section is called, was one of the most challenging and exciting whitewater runs in the eastern United States. More and more paddlers arrived each year to experience the river, and soon a small commercial rafting industry was established, guiding inexperienced but fit whitewater enthusiasts down the river. As boating traffic on the river grew, the Upper Yough became legendary not just for whitewater thrills but for its remote wilderness character.

Fortunately, it is now also possible to experience this section of the Yough on foot. An abandoned railroad right-of-way follows the east side of the river for almost six miles in an upstream direction,

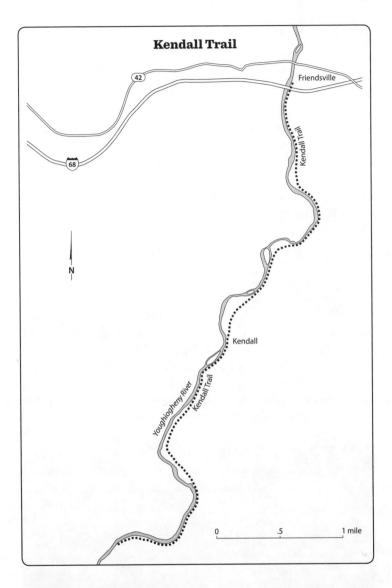

Kendall Trail

originating in the town of Friendsville, Maryland. Owned by the State and managed by its Department of Natural Resources, this trail provides relatively easy access to the river canyon and its superb scenery. Known as the Kendall Trail, it is named for a long-abandoned logging town located about two miles south (and upstream) from Friendsville.

Trip Description

Begin your walk at the green metal gate at the end of Morris Avenue in Friendsville; there is ample parking on nearby streets or in the municipal lot on Maple Street. The first two miles of the Kendall Trail are flat, wide enough to permit passage of an emergency vehicle, and there is often a gravel substrate. Nevertheless, in spring or after significant rains, the trail is frequently wet and muddy, as water drains off the surrounding hills toward the river. Friendsville residents use the path for exercise or dog-walking, so you'll encounter other hikers at all seasons. The first few hundred yards are noisy, as busy I-68 passes overhead on a high concrete bridge. Soon, however, the surrounding forest and high hills dampen that noise, and the only sound is that of birdsong, squirrel chatter, and the burbling whisper of the passing river.

The forest is dominated by oaks, hickories, and sugar maples, with occasional stands of eastern hemlocks on cool, north-facing slopes. The rail line was abandoned in 1942, and commercial logging ceased, so most of the trees are less than a century old. Still, autumn in the Yough valley is a colorful affair, dominated by yellows but punctuated by the occasional flaming red of a scarlet oak or red maple. There is an understory of witch hazel and mountain laurel, and sunny gaps in the tree cover permit herbaceous wildflowers like Joe-Pye weed and Turk's cap lily to thrive.

The abandoned townsite of Kendall is recognizable only as a wide flat spot in the landscape on either side of the trail about two miles from Friendsville. Kendall was founded in 1889 when a sawmill was established here. The surrounding hills were logged, the timber milled at Kendall, and the boards shipped out of the valley on the Confluence and Oakland narrow-gauge railroad. In its short-lived heyday, Kendall boasted a school, a church, and several houses. After a few decades, however, the timber had all been cut, and by 1920 the town was abandoned and the buildings torn down.

Just north of Kendall, the trail crosses a stream that has eroded the railbed, requiring a scramble over rocks filling the small defile. From this point on, the trail begins to narrow as the surrounding hills steepen and press closer to the river. Underfoot, the treadway becomes increasingly rocky. The trail also begins a steady uphill climb, mirroring the steepening gradient of the adjacent river. Rhododendron presses in on the trail, blooming attractively in June. Large boulders litter the hillside between the trail and river, while occasional shale-bearing cliffs provide deep shade and exude springs and seeps.

A cursory look at these shady, wet rock overhangs may reveal a dark green matlike covering that at first glance might be construed as algae. However, close examination reveals the most primitive land plant extant, liverworts. Liverworts are so primitive that they have not evolved a vascular system, so every cell must be bathed in water to avoid desiccation. The plant covers damp rocks as a thin, leaflike structure called a thallus, attached with rootlike structures called rhizoids. Under magnification, the thallus has a pebbled appearance. Its deep green color indicates a high density of chlorophyll, necessary to capture as much of the available sunlight as possible in these dark, shady habitats.

Should you hike the Kendall Trail on days when the Yough has sufficient water, take time to be entertained by the kayakers and rafters on the river. Above Kendall, the river gradient is so steep and the rapids so continuous that only experts can navigate the powerful churning whitewater as it passes over blind drops and through unobvious routes studded with dangerous rock sieves and undercut boulders. Few rivers require the skill, focus, and commitment that the Upper Yough does, and even fewer pass through such a rugged and remote river gorge.

The occasional whitewater kayaker will find the river too challenging and bail out, walking this trail downriver to Friendsville. Reports of "rattlesnakes" are common, although the herpetological identification skills of these already terrorized boaters is questionable. Nevertheless, hikers should stay alert for tubular reptiles of any variety sunning themselves along the Kendall Trail and avoid investigating the many crevices in the surrounding shale-bearing cliffs.

The trail narrows to a rocky footpath well above the river that is overhung with rhododendron in its final mile or so. It ends abruptly above a rapid called National Falls at a location where the railroad crossed the river on a bridge, now long gone. Return to Friendsville by the same route. Since the Kendall Trail is almost six miles one way, hiking its full length makes for a long day. However, you can turn around at any point, knowing that the final two miles will be a pleasant stroll on an easy trail.

Directions

From Baltimore or Washington, DC, take I-70 and then I-68 west, almost to the western border of Maryland. Take exit 4 and turn right on Route 42. Pass under the interstate, then turn right on Maple Street. There is a municipal parking lot on the right just before the road crosses the Youghiogheny River into Friendsville. The trailhead is less than a quarter mile from this parking lot; merely walk across the bridge, make an immediate right on Morris Avenue, and walk two short blocks to the trailhead.

Other Outdoor Recreational Opportunities Nearby

For those who enjoy difficult whitewater rafting, several outfitters in Friendsville offer guided raft trips on the Youghiogheny River adjacent to the Kendall Trail. This trip is for the very fit, very experienced rafter only. There are many hiking trails in Garrett County, but all are at least a thirty-minute drive from Friendsville.

"POISONOUS" SNAKES

Snakes, especially venomous ones, are viewed by a great many people with a curious combination of revulsion and perverse fascination. Our ambivalent attitude toward these tubular reptiles seems to be deep-seated but inexplicable. You may still not want to handle a snake after reading this, but a little knowledge and understanding of the life histories of snakes goes a long way toward building an appreciation of their role in the natural world.

There are only two species of venomous snakes in Maryland: the copperhead and the timber rattlesnake. Copperheads are found throughout much of the state, typically along mountain ridges, in rocky places, on stone walls, on debris piles, and in swamps on the Coastal Plain. Timber rattlesnakes are much less common and are confined to rocky mountains in the western part of the state and possibly a few isolated sites elsewhere. Both copperheads and timber rattlers are commonly called "poisonous" snakes, although that term technically refers to snakes that are toxic to ingest rather than those that conduct venom into a victim through fangs or a stinger.

Both of these species are pit vipers, considered the most evolutionarily advanced group of snakes. Their pits, located halfway between the eyes and the mouth, are actually infrared heat sensors that can pick up temperature differences as small as 0.002 degrees between an object and its background. These pits are an important sensory organ aiding in nocturnal hunts. Although they are diagnostic in identifying a venomous snake, they may be difficult to see from a safe distance. Another way to identify them is by looking at their eyes. Pit vipers have an elliptical pupil; in nonvenomous snakes the pupil is round. The tongue of snakes is not just an organ of taste; it picks up chemical cues in the air. The tongue is then retracted and placed into Jacobson's organ in the roof of the mouth where these chemical signals are analyzed and from which the results are sent to the brain. These snakes give birth to live young in late summer.

Copperheads average about two feet long with a stout body, a broad triangular head, and hourglass-shaped bands of reddish

(continued)

brown along the body. The top of the head is coppery in color, as their name implies. A copperhead hunts on the forest floor, frequently camouflaging itself under dry leaves as it waits for prey to wander past. Food includes small rodents, birds, frogs, grasshoppers, and other large insects. Copperheads will almost always try to escape if challenged.

Timber rattlers are much larger, measuring from three to as much as six feet in length. Their bodies are thick, with a markedly triangular head. Rattlers are tan to yellow in color with dark, wavy bands over the body, although there is a dark phase of the species as well as considerable variation in coloration. Rattles on the tail act as a warning to predators; one rattle is added each time the snake sheds its skin, an event that occurs about twice a year. Rattlesnakes prey on birds and small rodents, especially deer mice. Rattlers are preyed upon in turn by raccoons, red-tailed hawks, black racer snakes, and probably foxes, mostly when the snakes are young. Humans are a major source of mortality; in addition to road kills, den sites have in the past been dynamited. There is no faster way to decimate a population of rattlesnakes than to kill them in their winter den. Rattlesnakes exhibit a strict den site fidelity; many such hibernacula have probably been used for thousands of years. A snake caught out of its den in cold weather will die.

Venom from snakes like copperheads and rattlers is injected from a set of hollow, recurved, retractable fangs in the upper jaw. It is a mixture of more than a hundred proteins that dissolve tissues and nerves; a number of them have been isolated and are used by modern medical science. Not all bites from a venomous snake include injection of venom, and the amount of venom injected is highly variable. Nevertheless, any venomous bite is painful, and a severe one can be life-threatening. Although about 8,000 venomous snake bites are reported annually in the United States, only about eight to fifteen are fatal.

Snakes play an important role in maintaining the balance of nature, especially in controlling populations of small rodents. There is no reason to fear, harass, or kill them; snakes are happy to be left alone. Coexistence with snakes is mostly a matter of adapting our attitudes and keeping out of each other's way.

Swallow Falls
State Park

County: Garrett

Distance: Just over 1 mile as described; circuit hike

Difficulty: Easy to moderate. Hilly; rocky terrain

Dogs: Prohibited

Why It's Special: A virgin hemlock forest surrounding a whitewater river gorge studded with cascades and waterfalls

More Information: Swallow Falls State Park, http://dnr.maryland.gov /publiclands/Pages/western/swallowfalls.aspx, (301) 387-6938

Street Address: 2470 Maple Glade Road, Oakland, Maryland 21550

GPS Coordinates: 39.499090, 79.418415 (trailhead)

S wallow Falls State Park, at 257 acres, is one of Maryland's smallest state parks, but it packs an incredible amount of beautiful scenery into that tiny parcel. It contains the highest true waterfall in Maryland, a significant tract of virgin forest, and the deep whitewater gorge of the Youghiogheny River. Swallow Falls State Park is a wonderful destination for a weekend of camping, sightseeing, and hiking.

The walk described here covers the most scenic parts of Swallow Falls. The trail forms a loop and is short; the total distance is only about 1.25 miles. Nevertheless, you should allot at least two hours and make your walk a leisurely one. Although the trail as described is unsuitable for strollers or wheelchairs, a short section running from the parking lot to the Muddy Creek Falls overlook is paved with gravel and has sections of boardwalk and is suitable for those with physical challenges.

Trip Description

The day-use parking lot, with about eighty spaces, is located about a quarter mile from the park entrance. There is a comfort station here with wheelchair-accessible bathrooms, drinking water, and a soda machine. Adjacent is a store with basic camp supplies and a few museum items on display. Begin your walk at the Swallow Falls Canyon Trail arch on the far side of the parking lot. You'll find maps of the trail system here as well as at a number of other strategic locations along the way.

Walk downhill on the gravel trail for about 50 yards, and then turn right toward Swallow Falls at the signpost. Here you enter a 37-acre virgin hemlock forest (with a few white pines), the only such never-timbered stand of forest in Maryland. The largest trees are more than 300 years old, and thus they were standing before the arrival of the European colonists. But not all the trees are that old and large; the forest contains hemlocks of all ages and sizes. In the deep shade and rocky, thin, acidic soil, the only seedlings that can survive and grow are those of other hemlocks. As the large forest patriarchs eventually die, these younger hemlocks will replace them. Thus even a virgin forest is a mixed-age stand of trees. In October 2014, Hurricane Sandy wreaked havoc on this forest, toppling dozens of trees and leaving many holes in the canopy. Such gaps that permit light to reach the forest floor are a normal part of the life of a forest, and in a few decades there will be little evidence of what we humans called a "catastrophic" event.

Continue on the main trail. Although a number of side trails branch off to the left, they shortcut the main trail and miss some of the best scenery. Notice how shady it is under the hemlocks. Summers are deliciously cool here, and winters are brightened by reflections off the snow. Because of the shade, there is no undergrowth of shrubs or wildflowers, except in a few places. Invariably, this is where a hemlock has fallen, leaving a hole in the canopy for light to reach the forest floor. The most common wildflower in such spots is wood sorrel, with shamrocklike leaves and white petals lined with pink.

The trail passes by several wet places where springs, seeps, and streams dampen the earth. These are superb places to look for salamanders, small amphibians that are more common in forests than is generally appreciated. Turn over rocks, logs, and other debris in muddy areas to find salamanders. Most are two to four inches long;

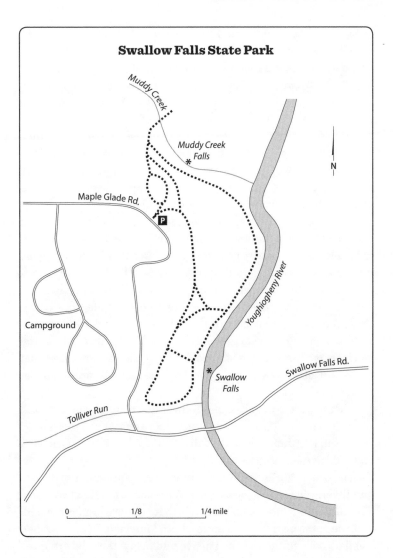

they do not bite. A fast hand is required, since exposed salamanders burrow quickly into crevices in the soil. Avoid handling salamanders for long, since they have the ability to discard their tails when threatened, and return them to their site of capture after examination. Replace the rocks and organic debris as well.

After about a quarter mile, the trail drops toward a small stream. It then turns left alongside Tolliver Run. The tiny stream has carved a minigorge for itself through the underlying rock. The creek jumps over a five-foot waterfall into a pool surrounded by a rocky amphitheater and overhung with hemlocks. The sandy beach at this sylvan scene invites a dip in the mountain pool, but the water is ice cold even in August and keeps out all but the hardiest souls.

Notice the rocks surrounding this pool; they form flat plates in horizontal layers. The rock here is a form of sandstone, a sedimentary rock composed of relatively coarse particles cemented together. As the name implies, the layers of sand formed atop one another at the calm edge of an immense inland sea, layer upon layer being deposited over time. This regular accumulation gives the rock its characteristic appearance as stacks of flat plates.

The rock strata here give a clue as to why all of extreme western Maryland is part of the physiographic province known as the Appalachian Plateau. It's hard to believe that this area is a plateau, given the high mountains and incised river gorges. But the flat layers of rock demonstrate that this whole upland was lifted as a unit, not tilted and folded like the ridges and valleys to the east in Allegany County, or compressed by heat and pressure like the Blue Ridge Mountains. Indeed, if you find a vantage point on a high ridge from which you can look out over a large section of Garrett County, you will see that the tops of all the mountains are at about the same elevation and that most are fairly flat.

The steep, rocky banks along Tolliver Run sponsor a lush growth of rhododendron. This woody shrub with leathery, evergreen leaves blooms in late June and early July. Its big, white, fragrant flowers lend a festive atmosphere to the trail.

The trail bears left as Tolliver Run tumbles into the Youghiogheny River. Within 100 yards, the river reaches the lip of Swallow Falls, a sloping, 25-foot-high cascade that is a focal point for hikers and one of the best-known landmarks in Maryland. In the summer, the flat rocks in the riverbed above and below the falls are filled with sunbathers, and if the river is low there is good wading in the deeper pools. Wintertime makes the falls a fairyland, as spray builds ever-higher fountains of ice over the rocks. And the fall color here is among the best in Maryland, as the reds and yellows of the sugar maples contrast sharply with the dark green of the hemlocks.

Just downstream from Swallow Falls is a large sandstone plinth called Swallow Rock. In colonial times, large numbers of swallows nested on the protected cliffs, giving the area its name.

Muddy Creek Falls

The trail follows the river downstream. Now called the Canyon Trail, it is narrower and more broken underfoot. In places, giant slabs of sandstone overhang the trail, as hikers scramble nervously to get out from under them. A few trailside boulders feature fossil tree trunks.

After about a half mile of such outstanding scenery, the trail almost imperceptibly leaves the Youghiogheny River. But the sound of water music is never far away, as the trail heads uphill alongside Muddy Creek, a tributary of the river. The trail soon opens to give a view of Muddy Creek Falls, at 53 vertical feet one of Maryland's tallest waterfalls. A stairway leads up the cliff face alongside the falls through gardens of wildflowers bathed in eternal mist. The top of the falls is a broad, flat rock where most visitors are tempted to see how close they can come to the edge. What is most mysterious is that such a wide, white curtain of water can come from such a tiny volume of water in the streambed.

From the top of the falls, turn left into a broad, grassy area marking the site of a camp where Henry Ford, Thomas Edison, Harvey Firestone, and the writer-naturalist John Burroughs met in August 1918 and again in July 1921. Western Maryland was a popular summer tourist destination even then, and many of the famous personalities of the day escaped the heat and humidity of Washington, DC, to visit inns and summer homes near Oakland.

The trail returns uphill to the parking lot, less than a quarter mile away, passing through more fine hemlocks, on a path that is paved with gravel (with boardwalks over wet spots).

Directions

From Baltimore or Washington, DC, drive to Deep Creek Lake in Garrett County. From Deep Creek Lake, continue south on Route 219. After losing sight of the lake, the first major road on your right will be Mayhew Inn Road. Turn right and go 4.2 miles. At the stop sign, turn left on the Oakland–Sang Run Road. Go 0.4 mile and turn right on Swallow Falls Road. Continue 1.2 miles to the park entrance.

Other Outdoor Recreational Opportunities Nearby

A five-mile hiking trail connects Swallow Falls State Park with nearby Herrington Manor State Park, where there are a swimming beach and canoe and rowboat rentals. Cranesville Swamp Preserve is only a ten-minute drive from Swallow Falls and is well worth the trip; it is described elsewhere in this book.

BLACK BEARS IN MARYLAND

For the typical Maryland resident, there is probably no wildlife sighting more noteworthy than that of a black bear. At the same time, relatively few Marylanders have actually observed a black bear in its native habitat. In part, the reason for this is historical; in the mid-1950s, there were fewer than a dozen bears living in Maryland. But for the most part these intelligent and adaptive mammals are rarely seen because they don't want to be; naturally shy and elusive, they have learned that interaction with humans can be stressful, harmful, or even deadly. For this reason, hikers who encounter black bears on Maryland trails often see merely the south end of a north-bound bear, for just a few seconds before the creature tops the next hill.

Black bears, the only species of bear native to Maryland, were fairly common throughout the state before its settlement. The extensive tracts of mature forest that covered most of the state constituted prime habitat, providing a plentiful supply of tender grasses and herbs in spring; roots, fruits, and insect grubs in summer; and mast in the fall. With no significant predators, bear populations were limited only by the food supply. With the coming of the colonists, however, bears were quickly hunted to the brink of extinction. The state legislature voted to approve bounties, and hunters like the legendary Meshach Browning prowled the woods secure in the knowledge that they were not only doing their civic duty but also making the land safe for settlement. Only a few of the most wary and elusive bears hung on, in deep, impassable swamps or on large tracts of forest in Garrett County.

Hunting was banned in 1949, and the black bear was listed as a state endangered species in 1972. As a result of these actions, as well as efforts to restock bears in the surrounding states of West Virginia and Pennsylvania, numbers of bears slowly began to rise. A resident, breeding population was established in Garrett County by the mid-1970s. Human-bear interactions, including road kills, nuisance complaints by farmers and beekeepers, and reported sightings increased rapidly. Bears were removed from the endangered species list in 1980, and in 1985 they were made a forest game species with a closed hunting season. Department of Natural Resources biologists estimated the black bear population in Maryland in the year 2000 at about 260 to 440 animals. That number increased to 700 within another decade. Most are found in Garrett and western Allegany Counties, on the high, forested Appalachian Plateau. There is a smaller, more fragmented population in Washington and Frederick Counties, and almost annually a juvenile male wanders eastward to the fringes of suburbia and into the local news. In 2016 Maryland had a banner year for such wandering juvenile black bears; there were sightings in all the Maryland counties west of the Chesapeake Bay. Bears were even seen on the busy campuses of the

(continued)

University of Maryland, College Park, and the Community College of Baltimore County, Catonsville.

Female black bears breed in midsummer and give birth while in the winter den in January or February. Three cubs per sow is typical for Maryland bears; at birth the cubs weigh only about eight ounces. Their eyes open after thirty to forty days. When they leave the den by early April, cubs weigh five pounds. Throughout the spring and summer, the family wanders across a home range of several square miles, the cubs gradually learning to feed themselves and find food. They are weaned by eight months and shortly thereafter spend their first full winter with their mother and siblings in the den. By their second summer, cubs are on their own, although sexual maturity takes three years. Bears' life span in the wild is probably about twelve to fifteen years, although zoo specimens may live up to twenty-five years.

Bears are not true hibernators; their pulse and respiration are almost normal in winter, and they will respond (groggily) if disturbed. However, their digestive system shrivels in winter and is blocked by a hard anal plug. During the rest of the year, bears avoid human contact by being mostly nocturnal; bears in true wilderness are much more active during the day.

As the populations of both black bears and humans have increased, contact has become more and more frequent. For example, between 1995 and 2003, 179 bears were killed by motor vehicles in Maryland. During the same period, complaints from homeowners in western Maryland increased dramatically; many feared for the safety of their children, pets, and property. If homeowners merely stored garbage in bear-proof containers and kept pet food and bird seed in safe locations, however, bears would have no reason to come around, and conflicts could be minimized. Nevertheless, homeowner and hunter pressure on the state legislature led to a recreational hunt of black bears in 2004. Over the ensuing decade, an average of sixty-five bears were killed by hunters each year, about 10 percent of the bear population. While this number permits a sustainable population size, the hunt is still controversial; many Marylanders who vacation in Garrett County would love to be able to see a wild black bear roaming free in its native habitat.

Cranesville Swamp Preserve

County: Garrett

Distance: About 1 mile as described; circuit hike

Difficulty: Easy. Almost flat; boardwalk through the swamp portion

Dogs: Prohibited

Why It's Special: Maryland's premier frost pocket bog, harboring unique plants in a remote mountain setting

More Information: The Nature Conservancy, https://nature.org /ourinitiatives/regions/northamerica/unitedstates/maryland_dc /index.htm (301) 897 8570

Street Address: near 4188 Cranesville Road, Oakland, Maryland 21550

GPS Coordinates: 39.532341, 79.486337 (trailhead)

Far out on the extreme western edge of Maryland, where the winters are long and the people few, lies one of the most interesting and unique natural places in the state. Cranesville Swamp, owned by the Nature Conservancy, harbors dozens of species that are rare or threatened or that exist nowhere else in Maryland. A visit to Cranesville elicits the feeling of the great north woods of Maine or Canada, with spruce trees outlined against the sky and tundralike vegetation underfoot. The hike described here is not a long one, but it should not be missed if you're vacationing at Deep Creek Lake or visiting state parks in Garrett County.

Cranesville Swamp occupies a low, bowl-shaped depression in the highlands of the surrounding Appalachian Plateau. Streams drain off the hills, and their waters accumulate in the valley because the underlying substrate is impermeable. Since the water has nowhere to go, the soil remains saturated year-round, promoting the growth of only those species that can exist in perennially moist, nontidal wetlands, called bogs. Furthermore, the low average yearly temperature prevents the growth of wetland plant species characteristic of other parts of Maryland. For this reason, Cranesville and a few other smaller bogs in Garrett County are referred to as "frost pocket" bogs.

When the last ice age ended about 12,000 years ago, the climate of Maryland was considerably cooler than it is now. Boreal forest dominated the land, including such trees as spruce, fir, and tamarack. As the ice cap receded, temperatures warmed, and vegetation better adapted to this more benign climate replaced the boreal forest in most of Maryland. Only in such high, cold places as the river valleys and frost pockets of Garrett County could remnants of the boreal forest hang on. For this reason, the vegetation of Cranesville resembles that of more northerly latitudes.

The walk described here is only about a mile in length. Nevertheless, allow at least two hours to observe the plants and enjoy the solitude. A 1,500-foot boardwalk makes the bog accessible and holds down human impact on the fragile flora. Cranesville Swamp was declared a National Natural Landmark in 1965.

Trip Description

Park your car in the small lot established for visitors. There are no facilities here at all, so arrive prepared. The trail to the bog is marked by blue blazes and is found at the far end of the lot next to an information board. Initially, the trail is partially open to the sun, so the undergrowth of mountain laurel, small trees, and bracken make thick going. Bracken is a sweet-smelling weedy species that grows in disturbed areas of the north woods. It is easily recognized as a coarse, upright fern up to two feet high with three regularly arranged horizontal leaves. Within 100 yards, the trail enters a plantation of planted trees, including red pine, Norway spruce, and Scotch pine; the heavy shade here reduces the undergrowth. Finally, the trail drops down a slight hill and emerges into the open bog, about a quarter mile from the parking lot. A boardwalk here permits dryshod exploration of Cranesville Swamp.

As you enter the swamp, scan the area for wildlife. You may surprise wary resident animals like a white-tailed deer, great blue heron, hawk, or owl. Once you leave the shelter of the surrounding forest,

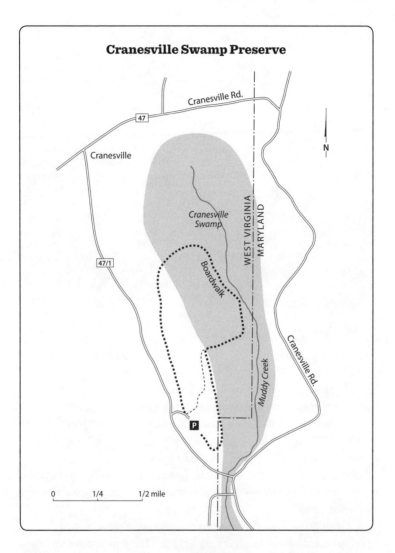

Cranesville Swamp Preserve

Cranesville Rd.

47

Cranesville

WEST VIRGINIA

MARYLAND

N

Cranesville
Swamp

47/1

Boardwalk

Muddy Creek

Cranesville Rd.

P

0   1/4   1/2 mile

you're much more likely to be spotted by these and other such shy animals. Among the breeding birds found in Cranesville that are officially designated as "rare" are the Nashville warbler, alder flycatcher, and saw-whet owl. Among mammals, black bear and bobcat frequent the swamp, although your chances of seeing one of them are slim. More diminutive but equally rare is the northern water shrew, a tiny but ferocious carnivore that feeds voraciously on insects and amphibians.

As you enter the swamp, a squarish pit with tannin-stained, open water marks the site at which peat was mined from the bog at some time in the past. Virtually all boreal bogs like Cranesville are underlain by thousands of years of the accumulated, compressed vegetation known as peat. Mostly sphagnum moss, the dominant plant of the open portions of the bog, peat is formed when each year's growth dies back. The extreme acidity of the water in a bog, however, prevents the microbial growth that causes decay, and peat accumulates to a depth of many feet. The pit is a good place to look for frogs and salamanders, as well as aquatic insects like whirligig beetles and water striders.

About 50 feet out from the woods, the boardwalk passes over an area where the vegetation is very low, and there are even patches of open mud. This is a fine place to get down on hands and knees and examine the surface of the bog. Sphagnum moss occupies most of the surface in a dense mat; in wet areas, it is possible to push down on one section with a hand or foot and see the ripple spread out over the surface, similar to the effect when a pebble is tossed into a lake. Although a bog may look solid, it definitely is not.

In addition to sphagnum moss, another common plant is the wild cranberry, a trailing vine with half-inch-long, elongate leaves spaced alternately. Their fruit becomes ripe in October, when visitation to Cranesville bog increases dramatically. Cranberries host one of the rarest insects in Maryland, the bog copper. Females of this little orange and black butterfly lay eggs on cranberry leaves; the larvae that hatch out feed on the juices of the leaf.

A common but minuscule plant can be found here as well. Look for tiny sundews on muddy, clear spots on the bog surface. These "carnivorous" (actually insectivorous) plants are much smaller than most people expect; many of them are less than an inch in diameter, so you will need to look closely. Leaves are circular and covered with glandular hairs that secrete a sticky substance capable of entrapping small insects. The leaves then secrete enzymes that digest the animal in place. The sundew derives nutrients, especially nitrogen, from the decomposition of the insect.

Patches of shrubs and even small trees form islands in the open parts of the bog. These represent areas where soil has collected around hammocks of vegetation, and the microhabitat is a bit drier than that on the surface of the bog. The buildup of higher, drier areas becomes a self-perpetuating occurrence and can lead to a gradual reduction of open bog over time.

The boardwalk leads into a central part of Cranesville Swamp where trees have established themselves. It is from this wooded portion of the preserve that Cranesville gets its official name of swamp. The term *swamp* applies to any wooded wetland; a *bog* is more limited, referring to a peat-filled wetland with acidic water. Hemlock, black spruce, and red maple dominate the swamp, but the rarest tree is the tamarack (also known as larch). One of the few deciduous cone-bearing trees, it has short, yellow-green needles that are found in clusters of twenty or so. The easiest time to locate a tamarack is in late autumn, when its needles turn yellow before falling. Only a single tamarack is easily observed from the boardwalk; it is found to the right about 100 feet off the boardwalk as it enters the tree zone.

The boardwalk ends in a beautiful, sun-dappled meadow of grasses, sedges, and cinnamon fern under several pines. The trail continues as a muddy footpath shaded by red maples, river birch, and hemlocks, with a dense understory of shrubs that encroach on the treadway. Fight your way through the vegetation as the trail encircles the open swamp, eventually reaching the junction where you first entered the bog proper at the start of the boardwalk.

From this point there are three trails that lead back to the parking lot. The blue trail is the one you came in on, the white trail is minimally maintained and difficult to follow, and the orange trail traverses new terrain through the upland forest surrounding the bog. I recommend the orange trail, a shady path notable for its abundance of non-flowering plants. Dry soils here have been colonized by three kinds of *Lycopodium*, commonly known as crowsfoot or running pine. With scalelike leaves, these simple but evolutionarily successful plants reproduce vegetatively using runners and sexually by the production of spores (but without flowers). Ferns are also common along this trail; there are extensive stands of hay-scented ferns and scattered individuals of Christmas ferns and cinnamon ferns. After about a quarter mile, the orange trail ends at the dirt road near the parking area; bear left to reach your car.

Biting insects are surprisingly absent at Cranesville. A few mosquitoes or deerflies may be present in the early summer, but in general you will not need insect repellent.

Directions

From Swallow Falls State Park (see previous entry), turn right on Swallow Falls Road. Go 1.35 miles, and turn right on Cranesville Road. Go 4.25 miles. Turn left on Lake Ford Road, which soon turns to gravel. Go 0.35 mile; bear right at the fork. Continue for about 200 yards, cross a small creek, and make an immediate right under the power lines. The parking lot is about 100 feet ahead. All these turns are marked with signs directing visitors to the "swamp" or "nature preserve." This parking lot is actually in West Virginia, as is the boardwalk; the border between the states runs through the middle of Cranesville Swamp.

Other Outdoor Recreational Opportunities Nearby

Swallow Falls State Park (described elsewhere in this book) is just a few miles from Cranesville, and it offers a beautiful hike through different scenery. Herrington Manor State Park is also nearby, and it has hiking trails, a swimming lake, and rowboat and canoe rentals.

"CARNIVOROUS" PLANTS

Bogs like Cranesville are some of the most unusual and inter-esting habitats in Maryland. To many people, however, a bog conjures up a variety of unpleasant images: clouds of pernicious, biting insects, disguised patches of sucking, quicksandlike mud, and malevolent carnivorous plants that reach out to kill unsus-pecting animals. All of these misconceptions, however, have scant basis in fact. Take, for example, the so-called carnivorous plants. Although this name has stuck in the public imagination for such organisms, "insectivorous plants" might be a better one. These plants obtain some of their nutrients by the capture and digestion of small insects; their prey does not include any of the vertebrates.

The most common of the carnivorous plants in North America are sundews, bladderworts, pitcher plants, and Venus flytraps. Only the latter is not found in Maryland, being confined to the Carolinas. The other species are rare, however, and are found only in specialized habitats like bogs.

Sundews, pitcher plants, and bladderworts all share certain characteristics. Each of them captures insects, primarily as a way to obtain nitrogen for the manufacture of protein. Nitrogen is usually a limiting factor in bogs; it is present in soils at levels in-sufficient for the proper growth of many plants. Sundews, pitcher plants, and bladderworts all attract insects to a chamber from which escape is difficult. Once an insect is captured, digestion is accomplished by the release of enzymes that break down its soft parts (although digestion by bacteria also plays a role in decom-position of the animal).

Sundews are the most common insectivorous plant in Mary-land. They are found in most bogs, whether those bogs are in the extreme western part of the state as at Cranesville or on the Coastal Plain of the Eastern Shore or southern Maryland. The plants are tiny, in some cases less than an inch across, and require observation on hands and knees (sometimes not an easy thing to do in a bog). The insects are captured on the surface of modified leaves, which are arranged on short stalks in a basal

(continued)

rosette. Each leaf has a number of hairs, and each one is tipped with a sticky substance that sparkles in the sun. When an insect lands on the leaf pad, it becomes entangled in the goo and eventually dies. The sundew flowers in June, although, in keeping with its inconspicuous nature, a hand lens is required to see any detail.

Bladderworts are less well known than the other insectivorous plants, but in some places they are more common. They tend to be found near open water because they capture swimming rather than flying prey. A small bladder is found on the surface or just under the water. When an insect touches the trigger hairs, a trapdoor on the bladder swings open, water rushes in, and the insect is swept along. The trapdoor closes behind, and the insect is eventually digested.

Finally, pitcher plants are the largest of our insectivorous plants. Their leaves are modified and fused to form a series of upright tubes with an attractive, mottled appearance. The interior of the tube is very slick, with downward-pointing hairs. Insects may fly or crawl in, but many cannot get out. Eventually they fall into the mix of rainwater, bacterial sludge, and enzymes in the bottom and die. The pitcher plant flowers in June, putting up a large, conspicuous, liver-colored flower.

Insectivorous plants are uncommon but great fun to study and enjoy when found in these unusual bog habitats. Together, these plants compose a fascinating and unique addition to our natural heritage.

Index

This index lists places, organisms, and concepts to which significant coverage is devoted in the text. It is not a listing of every occurrence of a word. Trip names are listed in boldface type. Illustrations in the photo gallery are indicated by "*color plate.*"